THE MARK

A REAL SALES GUY APPROACH TO SELLING CORPORATE ACCOUNTS

BRYAN J. SECK

authorHOUSE®

AuthorHouse™
1663 Liberty Drive
Bloomington, IN 47403
www.authorhouse.com
Phone: 1-800-839-8640

© 2011 Bryan J. Seck. All rights reserved.

No part of this book may be reproduced, stored in a retrieval system, or transmitted by any means without the written permission of the author.

First published by AuthorHouse 6/3/2011

ISBN: 978-1-4634-0428-4 (sc)
ISBN: 978-1-4634-0427-7 (hc)
ISBN: 978-1-4634-0426-0 (e)

Library of Congress Control Number: 2011908652

Printed in the United States of America

Any people depicted in stock imagery provided by Thinkstock are models, and such images are being used for illustrative purposes only. Certain stock imagery © Thinkstock.

This book is printed on acid-free paper.

Because of the dynamic nature of the Internet, any web addresses or links contained in this book may have changed since publication and may no longer be valid. The views expressed in this work are solely those of the author and do not necessarily reflect the views of the publisher, and the publisher hereby disclaims any responsibility for them.

For my beloved wife Alexis, my soul mate and mother to my two children. She is the rock of my family and without her I would never have done this book. For my Mom and Dad who never gave up on me during my wild teenage years, sorry for all the grey hair. Finally, for Stephen "Mr. D" Dyer, the first sales manager who hired me out of college when no one else would give me a shot at sales because I didn't have experience. Mr. D taking a chance and hiring me changed my entire life and where I am today. I hope I haven't let you down. Thank you, and I love all of you.

TABLE OF CONTENTS

Introduction ix
1   Real Sales 1
2   Real Selling vs. Let Me Throw Up on You 13
3   Eating Chickens While Hunting Elephants 17
4   Being a Thought Leader 25
5   Research, Research, Research 27
6   Letters, Emails, Phone Calls, Oh My! 37
7   Bridging the Gap 55
8   First Appointment 61
9   Validation Meeting 65
10 Second Appointment 69
11 Pricing 73
12 Referral Dos & Don'ts 77
13 I'm Out 83
14 Watch Your Back 87
15 Value Your Time 95
16 Final Thoughts 99

INTRODUCTION

The fact is that most salespeople are bad at selling. Only 3% are great, the other 97% are all doing the same thing, the stuff you read about in all the other sales books and training seminars. I wrote this book because I was tired of no one properly explaining what to do to get into, work, and close big accounts. I've sat in numerous corporate sales training classes, read all the sales books out there, and realized that most of the people who are teaching or writing about sales haven't sold in ten to twenty years. I'm amazed they even sold back then.

I am selling now, even as you read this book. I go after the Fortune 500 space with no prior relationship within the companies, and I get in the door at the C-Suite (CEO, CFO, COO, CIO, etc.) or the EVP/SVP level a majority of the time, no matter what I'm "selling." Why is that? In the coming chapters I will share some tricks of the trade with you on how I penetrate these large global organizations. If you're already working at that level then I'll show you ways to possibly improve or add to your approach.

Let me be clear from the start, there is no one paint brush in sales, no magical approach that works every time. Sales is a living, breathing process changing all the time, and we must change our approach to meet the different needs of each prospect. There's no one book that has the master plan to close every sale. If you could buy one book and use it and be successful every time then everyone would be in sales, and one author would be unbelievably rich. This book does not claim to be a sales bible or a how-to book for all salespeople in all industries. This is a book about real sales to corporate accounts. It is meant to stimulate your thinking about the sales approach you use, particularly when trying to access Fortune 500 companies and global corporations, and give you ideas to improve your technique. The tips in this book are based on what I have personally used to be successful in sales, not ten years ago but today, and I give you real-life examples to demonstrate how the techniques work first-hand.

In Chapter 1 we look at what I mean by "real sales," and Chapter 2 discusses some of the mistakes salespeople make in their sales approach. Chapter 3 will help you balance your desire for the big corporate sale with the necessity of smaller sales to pay the rent. Chapter 4 takes a look at how to lead the sale by being a thought leader for the prospect. Chapters 5-13 walk you through the actual steps of the sales cycle for corporate accounts, including research, calls, appointments, pricing, and referrals. This is where you'll find out how to get your foot in the door and keep it there. Chapter 14 takes a look at the different obstacles real salespeople have to watch out for, and Chapter 15 will discuss how to value your time as a salesperson. Chapter 16 offers some final thoughts.

Thank you for buying this book, I am confident that even if you're already a part of the top 3% of salespeople you'll find a trick or two in here that makes it worth your while, along with a good chuckle. Enjoy, and tell your friends!

1
Real Sales

Most people think sales is about spin, or that it's about what is probably the most overused word in sales vocabulary: strategy. While these may play a part in the sale itself, they are not what real sales is about. They are merely a component of what a complex sale truly is. The real sale I'm talking about is making an appointment with an executive of a Fortune 500 company (having no relationship with them beforehand) and then walking the prospect down your sales cycle and closing the deal. This is real sales, this is where the money and the recognition are.

When selling to corporate accounts, most people view sales as selling to middle management, or to groups of people within the lower structure of the company such as committees, the procurement or IT departments, etc. I disagree. The first step to being a real salesperson is to understand what real sales is, where it takes place, and who has the ability to achieve it.

WAITING FOR THE SALE

I debate this with my wife all the time. When she was doing new-home sales she was convinced she was in real sales. During the housing boom a monkey could have written new home sales since builders had waiting lists of people looking to purchase new construction. Though I know my wife is good at building rapport and asking for the sale, what she considers real sales is not what I consider real sales. Here's the difference: she sits in a model home and waits for the prospects or potential customers to enter her model so she can show them the product, which they will hopefully purchase. Marketing has a big role in this. Most new home developments do a ton of marketing, like car dealerships with the balloons and all. The result is the same: my wife didn't have to go out and find the sale, the sale came to her. Let that sink in for a minute or so. If you don't have to go out and find the sale, if it comes to you, then you are not in real sales. This includes retail, car sales, inside sales, order takers, etc. I'm sure there is an art to the sale once they come to you, but that's not what this book is about. It's about going out and finding the opportunity, qualifying it, not wasting any time, and closing it.

The analogy I made to my wife's new-home builder President at a Christmas party (after a couple of cocktails) made his eyes get big. This donkey was trying to debate me on why his new-home salespeople were the best salespeople in the country. Mind you, this is when the housing market was booming. I explained to him that the boom would ultimately end and that most of his "best salespeople" wouldn't be able to sell a sandwich to a starving rich man once it was over. Wow, was I right. When doing new-home sales there are a fixed number of lots on which you can build a new house, let's say for this example: one hundred lots. Once the people come to your model and you sell all one hundred lots then the builder is sold out. There are usually several phases (Phase 1, Phase 2, etc.,) each with its own set number of lots. The earlier the phase, the cheaper the house is, so the customer feels like he's getting a good deal; there is incentive to buy early. This is all pretty cut and dry. If you are a new-home salesperson, the customers come to you. If they like the model home then they buy the lot, build the house, etc. This is what my wife and her boss considered sales.

So back to the party. The analogy I gave him is what real salespeople deal with every day. I told him to take a neighborhood; pick one, any one. You can play along as well, think of a neighborhood near you. Let's imagine it has one hundred homes already built out and completed; it's an established neighborhood. If the builder was involved in real sales, the company would tell it's salespeople to go sell ten of those homes in four months. As a salesperson for the builder, you have no relationship with any of the homeowners, but you have to knock on their door, introduce yourself, identify who the owner is, and convince them to move in 4 months (where to, you have no idea.) You have to convince them you are the person to sell their house, and by the way, the investment they may have already made may be lost by selecting you. Successful salespeople, does this sound like any deals you're currently working? This is true sales, when you have to figure it out as you go, fake it until you make it kind of thing. Over time you find out what works and what doesn't. When customers come to you they are already interested or have a need, you just have to figure out what that need is and how to position yourself and what you're selling to accommodate the need. In this case, the difference between real sales and what most people consider sales is the act of going out there, being proactive, and finding business rather than having the sale come to you.

I would love to have my customers come to me. I remember when I was a young sales manager (which I don't recommend, it's a lot like babysitting and there's less money in it; don't get sold on the career-path thing, that's how they get you,) I interviewed a young woman who said she didn't like cold calling, she wanted to be able to make $185,000 a year, but wanted the prospects to come to her and all she would have to do was make the sales presentation. I told her when she found that job to let me know so I could interview for it!

Peddling a Product

Here's an interesting sales model: pharmaceutical sales. Ex-cheerleaders in their twenties go around stocking doctor's offices with pharmaceuticals, and they love to stop in and offer lunch to the doctors or to the whole office. There's a reason a majority of them are young, attractive women. Most doctors are single men who work crazy hours and don't get to "date" as much. Hence a young attractive woman coming in and taking him out to lunch can easily make it appear as though they're on a "date." This is how she peddles her product. When her product is being used she has to come by more often and replace it, so in her mind she's "selling," and she gets paid more. This is "the shorter the skirt, the shorter the sales cycle" model. Everyone knows this in the sales world, I'm just the one with the balls to write about it. And this is another example of what really isn't a sale in my mind. You're pushing a product with no tangible need assessment or benefit for the organization, outside of the doctor personally.

I know there's a pharmaceutical rep reading this right now insisting she offers a service which helps thousands of patients every day and changes lives. This is great, but if the products were as great as they claim then the medical community would hear about them via grass roots, medical conventions, etc., and not through Cindy Short-Dress placing samples in a cardboard box for a doctor in a strip mall. Sorry, this is not real sales.

This sales model is also why the turnover rate for salespeople is so high in commodity sales or product-driven sales. If you know several salespeople or more who have left or gotten fired in the past quarter, they were most likely in commodity or product sales. This is the "throw everything against the wall and see what sticks" approach. In this product-centric sale you are going to be measured on activity as the key performance indicator. You'll have managers and directors telling war stories about when they knocked on a hundred doors and one call closed someone. They have to "sell" the dream to you in order for you to get out there and have the greatest activity or market penetration, all the while knowing that half of you won't be there in two years. That is the sales model and the model won't change for you, so you can either accept it or get out of it.

How does product or commodity sales compare to real sales? Well, if you are in commodity sales, don't bother considering yourself on par with solution selling or strategic selling. It's not even in the same ballpark as real sales to global organizations; sales which directly affect their SG&A at the executive level. This is the big stick sales I'm talking about. The difference between a product sale and a solution sale is usually defined by the level at which you'll be working within the account. If you are dealing in the mid-management level or are in a committee environment, request-for-proposal (RFP) process, going against competition, etc., then chances are the prospect views your solution as merely a product sale. I know you have to go through the motions even at the higher levels too, sometimes, but the goal is to be at the C-Suite level guiding the organization as a whole down the sales process and being a thought leader with them. Being a thought leader with your prospect means standing apart from what every other salesperson is trying to do, which is just selling their product. I'll talk more about how to be a thought leader in Chapter 4.

Product driven sales are: here's what you get, the speeds and feeds or bits and bytes, here's how much it saves you and here's the cost. Think about most product sales out there and what you end up talking about at the middle management level: detail. At the executive level you're not talking about how many licenses, how fast it is, what's the overtime rate, cost per minute, cost per page, etc. You're talking about how does this positively affect their organization, how does it help their customers, and how does this improve overall cost expenditures and operations as a whole? The details get figured out later down the sales process, but the conceptual sale happens before anything else. Laying the conceptual sale foundation is key to laying the bricks of the sale itself. Sound simple? It's not, most salespeople try to push their product without selling the concept first. What ends up happening is they spend a tremendous amount of resources and time on the sale opportunity, but because they didn't sell the conceptual vision of the deal first there isn't any actual opportunity. This happens all the time and is a simple step typically missed in the first sales call or first executive meeting. I will talk about how to avoid this mistake in Chapter 6.

Sales vs. Marketing

All bad salespeople go into marketing. This is a saying I truly believe, and if you're a top producer it should make you laugh as well. Be that as it may, I've never had marketing sell me a deal before; it's never helped close my biggest accounts and never gotten me through doors I haven't been able to open myself. So why is marketing the biggest objection for underperforming salespeople? I've heard the record play a thousand times. Salespeople are not producing, and when I ask them why, they claim it's because they don't have any marketing materials. Their company name, product or service isn't being marketed and they can't sell because of it. Really? I have yet to ever have a prospect call me and say, "I just saw your marketing slick, we have to meet." Never happens.

I'm sure some would argue that the marketing opportunity trade shows and things of that nature afford are essential to sales, however standing in a booth and having people come to you is not real sales. Remember the housing analogy? Customers are at the trade show for a reason, and as a salesperson your job is to simply figure out what that reason is. Real sales is done via grassroots efforts and word-of-mouth. It's networking with clients you've signed in order to gain more market share and dominate your field. Marketing slicks and collateral are good for leave-behinds, but that is exactly what they are; leave-behinds in the sales process. You need to be able to recognize this and understand that marketing literature is not how real sales people get, obtain and close business.

A great way to tell the difference is if you've been selling in the field recently. If you have and are a top producer, you know one of the best blow-offs a prospect can give you is, "Send me your information." This is the number one blow-off to get you off the phone. Prospects know the salesperson will probably not send the information, and won't follow up, either. Still think you're not in product sales? If a prospect gives you this blow-off, think of me pimp-slapping you and saying, "I'm approaching this sale like everyone else and what I'm selling is a product which can be written about and the concept sold all in a marketing slick. I am unnecessary." Scary, right? It should be.

The salespeople who say they need more marketing in order to be successful are the ones who will be in marketing very shortly themselves.

These are the salespeople who love to deal with the *seymore* prospects. *Seymores*, as I call them, are people who will always meet with you, but always want to see more information. This should be a red flag that they don't carry the weight to sign up for what you are selling. Most details of sales are handled in lower levels that typically have less buying and signing authority. Keep this in mind when trying to package up your marketing slicks to mail out. You could be wasting your company's money, throwing it away on the *seymore* prospects who will never buy what you're selling. Trust that you may have to send the information your prospect is requesting, but verify first why they need it. **Trust but verify** is something salespeople should do all the time, even when purchasing a sales book. Trust that the author knows what they are talking about and that their approach works in the real world; verify that they themselves have used this approach in the marketplace to sell something other than their book, training or seminar in the last year.

Take marketing with a grain of salt. Most of them were bad salespeople who couldn't sell, then they moved to marketing to tell salespeople what customers want in terms of promotions, literature, etc. Not sure I understand that model at all and how it got so successful, but it is what it is. So if you're someone reading this book who majored in marketing in college, you probably realized when you got out that there's not a lot of marketing jobs out there and now you're working a sales job "temporarily" until you find that marketing job. I'll help you along in this process; update the resume or don't sell anything and a vacancy is sure to pop up in the marketing division.

"When I Was in Sales"

I loved it when my former VP's in telecom used to come in and talk about how when they were my age they were closing fifteen deals a week and were the best at what they did. Really? Before the Telecommunications Act of 1996? Back when there were only two companies to choose from? Back when internet and email didn't exist? Back when companies didn't even have IT departments? If you remember all that and you're reading this book you could be one of those VP's, so wake up. Times have changed in every industry, every prospect, account, economy and competition. Let's take telecom for example; now there are hundreds of telecom companies, resellers, authorized distributors, the internet, email, social media, etc., etc. The list goes on and on. Don't get me started on the "software sales" people who came from selling mainframe systems and act like they invented the internet or something back in the old days.

I'm also baffled when I meet people either in the IT space, support center, operations, analysis and of course, marketing department. It amazes me that they always have to tell me they "did sales" some time in their past. And they always say this as though it gives them credibility. The first thought that comes into my mind when someone says this is, "You must have sucked at sales. If you'd done well in sales then you would still be selling. You can't just walk away from the ridiculous amount of money you make if you're a good salesperson; you become too accustomed to it. You didn't leave a high six-figure position to take an $85,000/year support role, did you?"

Perhaps you've been on a conference call strategizing about an account, when someone from your internal IT, marketing, operations, or logistics department starts interjecting about how they would sell or position the opportunity. When someone starts this I automatically think, "I will not listen to anything you say, and perhaps may do the exact opposite because you already had your shot and it didn't work out." It sometimes seems as though everyone wants to be in sales or a salesperson, but no one wants to take the risk we take in order to be in real sales. Talking about sales and getting out there and selling are two different categories. Which one are you in?

REAL SALES IS NOT FOR EVERYONE

Another misconception is that anyone can be in sales. I'm a true believer that people are born with the ability to build rapport, and that charisma is an innate talent that can't be taught. I've seen the worst salespeople in terms of style, structure, processes, etc., close the biggest deals. They were able to form meaningful relationships more quickly than their competition. Everyone knows of someone in their past or present at work who is the guy/gal everyone loves to grab a beer with. They make the night a lot more interesting and fun, and they seem to have a natural gravity that attracts everyone. These are the naturals; they don't have their salesforce.com updated, their funnels are not high and tight for next steps, and yet they seem to close more deals than anyone else. It's rare you find the perfect storm of both natural ability and a strong sense of structure around sales cycles to match it. When you do, this is the cream which rises to the top of all other salespeople; the top 3% of earners in sales. These are real salespeople, and not everyone is cut out to be one.

Whether you're a new salesperson or long-time hardened veteran of sales you should always ask this question: "Why am I doing this?" Really think about it, because the real sales life is full of innumerable rejections, travel with countless airports and hotels, endless presentation and RFP nights, disappointments, little to no job security, and never-ending stress. If you're doing it because you have a picture of a Porsche or Ferrari in your cubicle, you better get out of sales. Wake up! No one in the firm has that car in the parking lot, but your manager sold you so hard on how much money you can make that they want you to post it up in your cubicle to stay motivated, even while you're getting your balls kicked in on the phone.

You should be in sales to do one thing: to dominate. Be the best you can be, not just in your company, but in your entire industry. When your competition walks into your prospect's office, you want them to see your name and organization on the sign-in sheet and think "Oh Shit!" Yes, "Shit!" That's how you dominate your profession. That is how you get elevated to 3% land.

Real salespeople need more than just a desire to succeed, though. **A real salesperson has to strive to be different.** Why follow the same mold as everyone else? In sales if everyone is doing it, then it's wrong.

Be the stand-out in your field of expertise. Be creative, most C-Level executives are creative thinkers and want the same working for them. They want to see something creative and different come across their desk. Show them you have something unique that they have never seen or heard and you will get their attention. I'll discuss more ways to get ahead of the pack in Chapters 5-13, but if you're not ready to break the mold and be unique, consider a marketing job instead.

A real salesperson should also be professional, honest and have integrity. Have you ever tried shopping for a pool with pool company salespeople? Every company says the exact same thing and all of them use scare tactics. It's an awful experience that I hope real salespeople don't ever have to go through. I can sit through all-day tax seminars with a smile on my face and when people ask how I do it, I reply, "Because I've been to four pool company presentations." Always remember that people buy from people they like and trust. If you demonstrate your expertise in a professional manner while having passion and being completely honest with your clients, they view you as an advisor rather than a vendor. Most vendors look out for themselves and put the customer second, hence customers treat them like vendors. A salesperson they feel is putting their interest ahead of his own and his company's is an advisor and will be allowed to come in and work as a thought leader to help develop the corporate strategy.

In order to sell to the big sticks you need to carry one as well. Come to the party with confidence or don't come at all. People always buy from people who are perceived as experts and are passionate about what they're selling. Sometimes it's that simple. I've beaten many competitors even though I was the highest priced solution because I was deemed the most knowledgeable and was confident my solution was better than anything out there. This confidence breeds success, as long as you're not cocky about it. Real salespeople have a certain confidence about them, and it's hard to miss.

Real salespeople also know when to utilize the take-away approach with a prospect and when to value their time more than the lower titles in an organization. Knowing when to walk away from a prospect that is in "maybe" land is the best way to qualify how you are as a salesperson. Real sales people want a yes or no, that simple. If it's no, tell me so I don't waste anymore of my time. If it's yes, then let's really talk about the challenges your organization is facing and how my company can help. Think about deals you're working or have lost. Do you have to squeeze to get information from the prospect? Does it feel like they are controlling the sales cycle? How many times have you presented or met with a prospect and not received a solid next step? Do you hear things like, "We're still reviewing it" or "We still need to look at it?" If so, then you're not in control of the sales process. A real salesperson is always in control of the sale.

Real sales is about identifying and finding the opportunity. It's about being professional, trustworthy and working the prospect to the close stage. Real salespeople have a swagger which is confident but not cocky. This is especially true at the C-Suite level in the Fortune 500 space. Convincing an executive to select you without any prior relationship or knowledge of you is a high salespeople love to get. It's the thing that makes the thousands of no's okay and keeps you coming back for more.

2 REAL SELLING VS. LET ME THROW UP ON YOU

The first thing salespeople want to do when they meet with someone, especially the higher up the food chain they go in an organization, is to show credibility by presenting everything they can do. This is especially true in the software sales arena. I've been on a ton of WebEx's where the salespeople are so proud of their software and what it can do that they spend one hour talking and showing it off, while the prospect hasn't said one word. These salespeople always ask the dumb question thirty minutes into the call to make sure the customer is still on the line, "Am I going too fast or slow?" "Does this make sense to you?" These are inane questions that do nothing to move your sales towards the close.

This scenario is also very typical of start-up companies and family-owned businesses. They are so close to the product or service that they think telling is selling. How wrong they are! Prospects don't wake up in the middle of the night thinking about your solution, product or service. It just doesn't happen that way. Salespeople typically try to show as much as they can in order to say, "We can do this for you, we can solve your problem, here's why." This is the "let me throw up all over you" mentality. Good luck! I'd love to know what the company close ratio is under this approach.

For great salespeople, this is a waste of time. Know your prospect and what their goals are *prior* to doing the calls or demos. You can ask this simple question, "How do you view success as related to this demo?" Let them tell you their buying criteria, then you can determine if you meet what they deem to be success by the end of the call. You can pre-close them by asking, "Is it agreed that we can move forward if I'm able to make this demo a success from your standpoint?" And moving forward can mean a million different things: sales process, decision process, next step, final selection, etc. Have them tell you what *they* want to see, rather than you showing everything to them and hoping something sticks.

If you have a good coach in the account, do the demo for him prior to doing it in front of the group or his boss. Let him give you insight into what you should spend more time on, add/delete, etc. A good coach is someone within the company who will give you input and insight into what they are really looking for or the challenges they are facing. The coach is willing to help you because they have a true business problem or challenge they are trying to solve. If at the end he says everything looks good, then you know you have problems. Chances are if your coach doesn't have any input then they are not really your coach in the account. Or if no input is given, this should at least make you aware it is probably not a top priority for him or his peers and more than likely they are just "seeing what's out there." Remember, though you think he's a coach in the account he might be coaching his own internal people or your competition, as well. A coach can also try to sabotage your deal or presentation with a smile on his/her face. You could be the leverage for him to prove he is making the right decision with someone else or validate himself and his department to his boss.

If they are really looking to do business with you or really looking to honestly find a solution, then they need to have the same amount or even more involvement in the sales process. The coach needs to have a predetermined notion that these ideas are his, and he should have an understanding of how to guide you past the hurdles he may run into internally when trying to sell it up the food chain. The prospect or coach needs to have skin in the game and needs to feel like it's his ideas you molded into your solution, he needs buy in on his own ideas. This seems like a simple idea, but most people fail to remember it.

The other misstep most salespeople make in a sale is not identifying the stakeholders and not understanding the company's internal decision process and buying process. If you think back to some deals you have lost, chances are you didn't hit one of these or possibly all three. If it's all three, get into marketing, quick!

Take a look at these simple questions you can ask:

- What is their challenge/pain?
- What is their process to make a decision? Have they done this before?
- Are the people with the proper authority committed to act?
- Is there a budget for this project or will there be one?

These questions need to be asked on your first sales call, broken down to more complex open-ended questioning so you get an understanding of what they wish to accomplish (we'll get deeper into this in Chapter 8.) What most people don't realize is that you didn't bring your solution to the company out of the blue and then they bought it, never once looking at it or experiencing some sort of challenge around it.

Typically someone at the C-Suite level or executive level tells someone below him to look at this piece because of _____ (you have to find this out, and don't rely on what the underlings in the company are telling you.) Then this thought gets pushed down for investigation into the matter directed from the top. Typically, the next in line on the food chain pushes it down yet another level. Now here's where most salespeople start to get involved, around this level of middle management or even VP/SVP/EVP level. Tell me if this sounds familiar. A group is formed (committee or team), and the players are usually VPs, directors, managers, procurement, IT, etc. The same old players and the same old song. And what do all of these people want: detail. They want to know how, how much, timeframes, implementations, systems, etc. They want to see WebEx's, have meetings, get on conference calls, etc.

This is when most salespeople get excited; they think it's a hot prospect because they are able to meet with a bunch of people. So they meet with them, tell them all about their product and services, send proposals, pricing, etc. They throw up all over them, but most of the time they never get the deal. Why? **When you let the prospect control the sales process without you walking them down your sales cycle, it rarely pans out well for you**. What does happen is this: as a salesperson you spend a tremendous amount of time and company resources chasing this opportunity like a dog chasing its tail. And guess what else you're doing? Exactly what every other sales rep in America is doing; being led and not leading the prospect.

How often do you challenge the prospect on why they are meeting with you? It's a hard question to ask since you've worked so hard to get the appointment, but in order to be the best you have to ask what no one has asked them before. Albert Einstein once said, "If you do what you always did, you'll get what you always got." If what you're doing isn't working – do something different!

Some questions I ask prior to even going onsite are:

- What business results are expected from this investment?
- How will you measure success?
- How did the idea come about? Who had the idea?
- Will final recommendations be presented to the executive level?
- What did I say that grabbed your attention and granted me this meeting?

Again, these are simple questions, but they should shed tremendous light on whether or not your prospect is truly a prospect or just a waste of time. I understand it's hard to accept the truth; most companies you have in the "target" or proposing stage are not real opportunities, they are more like fluff to keep your manager off your back. But knowing when to walk away and not waste time is some of the best advice I can give any salesperson. I talk more about time management in Chapter 15.

The great salespeople are honest with what is in their funnel. For me, I have a whole process and model for working the large accounts, and when I hit every step, I've found that I have a high success rate for close. The highest Global Fortune 100 account I sold last year was a Fortune 5 account. I took the same methods I will show you here and had success. These are real life examples I will share that have happened in the last year or two. As mentioned before, you won't hear me talking about things I did 20 years ago or back when I used to be in sales because I'm now marketing my books full-time. I'm still selling what I sell.

3   Eating Chickens While Hunting Elephants

Time and time again I see salespeople only targeting the Whales or Elephants in their particular field. These are the big corporations, global enterprises, and Fortune 500 companies within each industry. Targeting them is great, after all we're in sales and the bigger the sale, the bigger the commission. We're in sales so we can land the deals that are life-changers. The problem is that many times these salespeople never seem to last at their companies. Why is this? Simple: they starve.

Elephants have a large complex sales cycle and have many complicated steps in the entire process. Thinking back to one of my largest sales, the sales cycle was over three years long. When your customer is going to spend $48 million a year with you over the next three years, it's a pretty big deal for them and for you as well. If I had solely relied on this deal I would not have been employed by my company for very long. The key is to balance the life-changers in your funnel with ones that will keep the lifestyle you're accustomed to moving forward. In the next several chapters I will talk more about penetrating the larger opportunities, for some of you these may be your elephants and for others they may be your chickens. Either way I'm confident there are ways to encompass the knowledge I'm going to share into both opportunities.

Elephants Like to Fish

When chasing the elephant you have to be conscious of time spent and the reward at the end of the month/quarter/year. The key is to be real with your elephant opportunity and challenge yourself to understand the true sales cycle and how you can lead this elephant to the close. I've seen many people who target elephants take appointments with large groups or with people who are not at a decision making level; appointments they wouldn't normally take. They do this because they are blinded by what the opportunity really is, they have dived into and believed their own hype. They get blinded by the big named account instead of looking at the titles they're meeting with. They tend to lie so much they actually believe their lies to be true. Don't fall into this trap; it will ultimately be your demise.

Think of the elephant as someone who goes out all the time to fish and see what nibbles it can get. Let's take a Fortune 100 company as an example (and all the names on this list are excellent prospects for any industry or service you are selling.) Typically in an enterprise or global acquisition many players have to be involved, and depending on the sale, the ultimate approver is usually pretty high up the food chain. Sales reps always bite at the first line that's dropped into the water and they forget it's just fishing.

Most of the time the elephants are fishing to pull up vendors. I use the word "vendors" instead of "partners" because the word "partnership" is used too loosely now. Partnership to me means someone who is willing to take a risk with you and your company to ultimately achieve the same goal; you sell and they use your expertise and services. Elephants are notorious for checking out current market conditions and doing their due diligence to make sure they are getting the best deal. Being such a large corporation it takes executive sponsorship in order to make a change. The risk to change is so high, they typically try to expand upon the services in which they are currently invested. This is why they tend to look into "other" solutions, but rarely make the enterprise wide "big" change.

Here's the common problem people have when being in the water with their competition or sharks. They try to fight over the bait on the line and the fisherman or corporate account is dictating the entire sales process. People tell me all the time, "I have to meet with them at this level, it's how they work." Really? I sold a Fortune 100 account that had as its corporate policy to go to RFP for anything over $1 million in annual cost. I was at the CFO level and convinced him my solution was the best for the challenges they were facing. I helped the CFO write a single source agreement between our two companies protecting him internally and circumventing the procurement process; all of this for $10 million in annual spending. Still think you have to follow their internal processes? The people who make the process can change it at any time, and when you deal directly with them you have direct influence over the process.

Also involved in the above example were two of my competitors. They were down at the VP level in a committee environment going through the RFI and soon to be RFP process. Do you think they had any clue what was happening at the top level? I would have paid good money to see their faces or be on the phone when the procurement guy all of a sudden went cold. How many hours/resources do you think they spent and wasted being at the wrong level?

Dancing for the Elephant

When you're in an elephant account, be aware. Sometimes you will have to do the dance and jump through some hoops. I've had to do it as well, where you meet other vendors and go through the process, but you have to separate yourself and this comes down to the natural ability or 3% I was talking about earlier.

I'll give you an example. The largest cigarette manufacturer in the world put out an RFP for services for a five-year contract and two-year option renewal, a seven-year contract in total. Everyone and their brother responded to the original RFP and my company was selected to be in the final three. My company lost the RFP and the notice of award was given, but it was public. Three months later this company's procurement person called our company and said it was going back out to RFP. I wasn't involved in the first response to the RFP but received the call from the procurement person. I wanted to respond; to me it meant the contract fell through during the terms and conditions stages. My VP at the time did not want me to respond because we had already lost it during the first RFP release. I wanted to respond, I had nothing to lose, and everything to gain.

No resources were given to me, no analyst and no RFP support, so I had to go solo. I spent three days working throughout the night responding to each RFP answer in my own way and not providing them with boilerplate responses, which are so common on RFP's. I quickly drew the conclusion that security played an important part of this tobacco company's decision making criteria, and for obvious good reason. They frequently get targeted by angry people who have lost loved ones to lung cancer. After I responded, they called the three vendors back for a Q & A session with the committee. Yeah, *the committee*, happy-happy-joy-joy. I hate these committees; why is it that the procurement guy always acts like he's the business owner? Let's be real, procurement's role is as the worker bee that forms the contract. I also love it when the procurement guy has a Napoleon complex, it's like a two-for-one deal and it makes me chuckle every time.

Anyway, I showed up to the Q & A and was running about twenty minutes late for the scheduled starting time (I'm always on time, this was rare for me.) I called ahead and let them know I was in traffic and would be running late. When I finally arrived at the facility one lady was waiting in the lobby for me, the SVP of the committee. I walked in, a young 27 year old (I'm 35 now) all by myself. I apologized for being late and shook her hand. She kept looking behind me as if more people were supposed to be with me. She asked me, "Bryan, are we waiting on other people from your company?" I told her no, it's just me. She said, "I'm a little concerned. The other two vendors have brought their VP's and have about eight or nine people each with them." I told her, "I'm a little concerned that VP's have the time to go to a vendor Q&A session, which should be able to be run by the salesperson who will be with you after contract signature and during implementation. I'll be able to answer any questions you have, and I have many myself." She was taken aback for minute, then said, "I never thought of it that way, I guess I'm a little concerned about that as well." Right then I knew I had it. Never even had to walk into the committee meeting. It was a quick sentence that changed the whole dynamic of the deal. That's how quick things in the elephant world can change; snap of a finger. The best part, I was right, as SVP she was the true business owner of the entire process. She was the decision maker, but not the approver, it still had to go up to the CFO for approval.

I drove the strategy of the account after that. When your customer gives you the keys to drive it's a great feeling. On the way out the other two vendors told me the decision was already made and I was "window dressing." I hope the VP of my competitor who told me this reads this book, Karma!! I ended up closing the deal and found out the original award had to be rebid because they did not originally involve their Finance department from the very beginning of the RFP process. I had a leg up because Finance automatically hated the original company they picked, it was political and Finance was flexing its muscle. When I found this information out during the process, guess whom I reached out to: that's right, Finance. I went around procurement, yes, breaking the law of "everything needs to go through procurement." I spoke with Finance on the phone and laid the foundation of my solution and their buy-in prior to even presenting my solution. This was key. When I presented my solution I had Finance in there selling for me.

This is something everyone needs to know: when dealing with elephants you only sell 25% of the deal. You will only be credited for 25% of the sale, because 75% of the sale happens when you are not there. When they have internal meetings, one-offs and internal conference calls about whom they are going to select, this is when your deal is sold. Most of the time, as much as we'd like to say it is us, it's someone on the inside who likes you and fights for you in these closed door meetings. In this example it was the Finance SVP and the business owner SVP with whom I built quick rapport; she felt I was an expert in my field. I was awarded the contract two weeks after presenting my solution.

Leaving an Elephant

Knowing when to walk away from an elephant is the hardest thing a salesperson can do - the takeaway. Sometimes your elephant isn't going to be a good customer, plain and simple. I worked a sale for a large financial company that makes appliances. They were doing a reverse auction bid. If you ever hear of this, RUN. This has clusterf@#! written all over it. In this reverse auction the procurement guy, or Napoleon, came into the room and said, "These are our terms and conditions, we're XYZ Company and if you don't like it you can leave." Does this sound like the start of a good partnership or are you going to be a vendor just like the other 500 vendors they use now? I got up and walked out, the only one to do so. I think it took everyone by surprise, but I realized my time is worth more to my customers than this donkey, I'm better than that. Even in that moment I could see the snickering of the other salespeople, but I didn't care, I'm silly like that.

I have no magic story here to say they were so impressed they called me back and I won the deal. They went with someone else and that's that. I had them targeted as one of my elephants, but quickly removed them from the list. I want to work with people who want to work with me and see my value. If a company selects you on price, they will leave you on price, it's that simple. I could tell the account was going to be high maintenance. Thinking back, everyone in the room heard and saw the same thing I did, why is it I was the only one to stand up and walk out? The 3%, I suppose. I figured I'd let them fight for the bait on the line and I would go out and try to hunt, kill and eat something on my own.

Don't Forget the Chickens

Whatever you're selling, value your time just as much as your prospect's. Chase the elephants, but be careful (shhhhhh, I'm hunting wabbits....) The key is to work the larger accounts but also target accounts which are in the sweet spot of what you do. For example, I sold some of my largest accounts in a sub market or B market as defined by my company. So while selling in Washington DC, I also sold in Richmond, VA. Know where you can play and be dangerous, it's not always in New York or Los Angeles. Many good companies have their corporate facilities in some smaller markets; look at those while you are trying to penetrate the elephant accounts. These smaller accounts or "chickens" are easier to close, have a much shorter sales cycle and you can leverage the people in these more for referrals (see Chapter 12). These are the ones that are small enough for you to have a substantial impact on and form some of your best relationships with. The people you sell in these accounts also move around the most from company to company; keep in touch with them. If you do a great job for them here and they go somewhere else it's an easy layup of a sale for you.

A word of caution on the chickens: don't go too small. Everyone has done this without fail, I don't care what industry you're in or what you're selling. You sign up the smallest account and they end up taking the biggest amount of your time. I don't know the reason for this, but it seems the accounts that net you the least amount of money seem the most problematic and take the most time out of your day. Just be careful you don't go down that rabbit hole, it's hard to get back out on good terms when this happens.

My advice is to work the elephants (this is why we are in sales,) but also work the chickens so you don't starve while hunting the elephants.

4 Being a Thought Leader

A thought leader is someone who understands the challenges a company is facing and helps to move them in a direction which may fall outside of their particular sale area. He understands the big picture of the organization and makes suggestions that are the best for his customer, suggestions they haven't thought of yet because they are not subject matter experts in that area. Let's use office equipment or printers/copiers/MFP's for a real life example. A typical salesperson who sells office equipment may get an account which has hundreds of copiers. The bigger the machine and the more "clicks" or impressions each machine makes, the more money the sales rep makes. A typical sales rep meets with the customer to discuss how they can swap out the customer's current copiers/printers for their own brand. They talk about saving money, blah, blah, blah. An example of someone who is a thought leader in this position would be a rep who looks at the utilization of these machines and asks the customer why they are printing out so much to this one particular machine. Can the process be automated? This goes against what he/she is selling and gets paid for, but it looks at ways to help the customer and it thinks outside the box.

Think about some of the RFP's you get, don't they all seem to follow the same format? Everything is the same to one extent or another. Salespeople are no different, and differentiating yourself is the key to success in any sales engagement. Salespeople who see other areas a prospect should be looking at, who expands the scope of the customer's vision because they know it will ultimately be what the customer is looking for, have established themselves as a trusted advisor and thought leader in the account. You have to know when to utilize your expertise to separate yourself from the competition, and have conversations with your prospect that may be hard to have. This differentiator, and helping to drive the end result your customers desire, can be game changers in the sales world.

I once presented to a very large holding company that owned and had about 82 other companies reporting to it. My prospect at the holding company tried to leverage their buying power for all 82 companies as a whole. The biggest challenge they faced was communication and politics between all the companies and the autonomy they each had. This wasn't going to be a mandated contract that the other 82 companies had to buy from. Most sales reps came in with their lowest pricing and offered the biggest discounts from the beginning. Not too much thought leadership happening. After talking to the prospect, we quickly agreed that carrying the same message to all 82 different companies would likely be the hardest challenge. Being a thought leader for them, I created a program called S.W.A.T. (Strategy With A Target). I walked them through how this SWAT team would consist of the same group of people going to all 82 companies to pitch to each of them. This would keep the message consistent and allow the reporting and feedback the holding company was looking to accomplish but weren't sure how. By creating this program and doing this simple thing, I became the thought leader in the account and was able to sign a majority of the 82 companies up for my services. My competition wasn't even having conversations like this with the prospect.

It's important to find out everything you can about the prospect and his challenges, and help guide the strategy as the subject matter expert. You have to ask yourself, if your prospect controls everything and knows more about it than you, why would they need you or bother to sign up with you? Positioning yourself to be the expert they need without realizing they need you is crucial to taking the lead role of thought leader. Having innovative thoughts and ideas to help their business run is an example of how you will separate yourself from the competition and dominate your industry as a whole. In the next chapter I'll start walking you through my process and share some of my secrets to selling global Fortune 500 companies. But not all of them, I still have to use them today to get into accounts just like you.

5
Research, Research, Research

I was no valedictorian, and my employers can validate that I hate using *salesforce.com*. Most great salespeople loath having to take time out of their day to do data entry for their companies so reports can be generated. You end up filling out Excel spreadsheets with the same information you just entered into the reports. It's a vicious cycle that every large sales organization seems to have. Even so, I am a true believer in research.

Research into your potential prospects is key to your success. The reason top C-Level people don't meet with salespeople is that they don't have the time to educate you on their business. Think about that statement for a minute. So far I've been telling you about time management and when to know when to walk away from a deal; executives do the same thing. Think about how they immediately try to back you into a corner to find out what you do. Their job is to figure things out and then delegate. They are the chief outsourcers of detail. They come up with a big idea like, "We need to cut SG&A by 10%." They don't tell you how, where, why, etc. This message then gets pushed down to the lower levels who are then responsible for figuring out how, where and why. This is the space in which most salespeople play. They usually get the information from the lower levels without knowing why or where it really came from. Then they run out and throw up all over the prospect all the things they can do. To set yourselves apart from these jokers, you have to know more. Knowledge is power in any form and any walk of life, sales is no different. When you are knowledgeable about their business you grab their attention better, you are different than everyone else. Think about it.

Understand the Numbers

So how do you become different and knowledgeable? You have to put the time in if you want to succeed. My first sales manager and one to whom I owe a majority of my success, "Mr. D," always had the best one-liners, and great life lessons as well. One of his great lines was, "Success is not your mission, it's your lifestyle." Priceless! Let's see if you're one of the 97% of regular salespeople: do you know how to read your prospects' financial reports? Do you understand when you listen to the Q Earnings calls? Are you even on the Q Earnings calls? Do you really know what the numbers mean? Really?

Most salespeople I know say they look at companies' annual reports and 10K's, but when I read the same reports I have a completely different understanding of where the business is and where they are trying to go. This is key; if you understand their challenges on the enterprise-wide level or macro level you can then position yourself to be a part of the solution, regardless of what product or service you offer. **Knowing and understanding their company is vital to having successful meetings with executives.** Most salespeople don't even understand the different numbers in the columns they're reading; they have no clue when it comes to income statements, balance sheets, statement of change in financial condition, etc. I'm not saying you should get in a pissing match with a Fortune 500 CFO about financials; you'll get out-classed every time. But you do need to know the language these executives are speaking if you want to even have an intelligent conversation outside of throwing up your product and services on them.

Remember, sell them without mentioning product, service or price. For 97% of you, this will be outside of your comfort zone, and that's a good thing. Most salespeople are just bad at what they do, or they buy into the hype with spin selling and seminars. In the real world, it's completely different. That's why most people can't get to the C-Suite on a list, or even to their gatekeepers.

Research allows you to go in and let the prospect experience a truly consultative sell. Consultative selling may be new for some of you, or you may think, "This is exactly how I sell," and that's great. You can always expand upon this or add some simple things to really stand out and be different. When you do the proper research you earn the right to speak with the executives; you're prepared and won't waste their time.

You'll be able to speak their company language. *They* won't have to educate *you*, *you* are here to educate *them*. Think about that statement and your last big meeting. Did you feel like they led the meeting, that they took control? You should be running and controlling the entire process with input from them. You are the expert who deals with this every day.

By doing research you will also know their key measurements (KPI's, Scorecards, etc.) This will also show you how they will evaluate your solution as to its success or failure, and ultimately if they will buy or pass on it. As I said, research allows you to speak their language. Prospects don't wake up and think about your product or service, however executives do think about things at the enterprise-wide level, like cash flow, revenue, SG&A, etc. If you can show them how your solution, product or service affects one of their problem areas and have them agree to the impact in a monetary number, you will close the deal every time. When you don't have some of these components then you'll lose it somewhere, but it all depends on the deal itself and the politics surrounding it as well.

I'm not going to discuss here how to read annual reports/10Ks/13-week calls/investor relation calls, etc. If half of the 97% out there buys this book then maybe my next book will be about reading company reports, both public and private. I feel a sequel coming!

DIG FOR INFO

When I'm planning on penetrating a large account I take time to do all of my research prior to even making a phone call. Here's what I do, which has worked well for me. I qualify the opportunity in my space; any Fortune 100 account is a potential customer outside of the ones I have already sold. I start my research on the company website and internet first. I check to see what the latest news with the company is, what's the latest and greatest. I then look at investor relations. This is where they want you to buy into their company, so there is a lot of great fluff they use that you can use on them later down the road; trust me on this it works. C-Level executives always want more investors, when their stock goes up so do their bonuses and equity in the company. I play this card quite a bit with a tremendous amount of success. The biggest compliment I've ever had was during a shareholders meeting when a Fortune 100 company CEO discussed my solution and how it affected and reduced their SG&A to shareholders. This is exactly what I put into his brain on my first call and fourteen months later he was saying it. What a great feeling, let me pause while I pat myself on the back. Ah, memories.

Moving on, after I review the company website I do research on the company governance, executives and board members. I go through their annual reports, look at their business strategies to see what they target and how they measure success. It's essential to understand what they do as a business. Think about the prospect from their point of view. How would buying something from you affect them and how they sell to their customers? If you can answer this question then you're ahead of the game. Remember, they're in business to make money too, and if you can show them how to be more efficient or productive they will buy from you, especially if it will result in more revenue from their customers.

To the best of your ability you have to try to understand their principal lines of business and where they are. Many global organizations have underlying companies and reporting structures. Think of the automotive industry and how many different lines of business and sub-companies there are under the umbrella of the larger company. This is particularly relevant with holding companies and global enterprises.

Understand who your prospect's customers are and how what you are selling will give them a competitive advantage in terms of those customers. Leveraging this is something people often forget. **Always remember that they are here to make money just like you, so show them how they can make more money *with* you.** Most salespeople try to show ROI or how to reduce costs. Have you ever sold a deal where you were the most expensive option, or way more expensive then what they currently had? Chances are they valued how your solution would help them with their customers. Supply-chain management and manufacturing are ideal for this. I've sold some of my biggest deals by showing them how to increase their customer base and revenue. It's an art, and you have to get agreement for it to work, but when it does, its gravy.

I also look at the challenges my prospects are facing. Whatever you do, when you first meet with someone do not ask, "What *problems* are you facing today?" I prefer the word "challenge" to "problem," it's more positive. And you should already know the answer to this if you've been doing your research. Instead, you should position it as, "I've noticed one challenge you face is moving from the old production model to the new service model as outlined in last year's report. Cost for this new model went up 32%, how has this affected your customer base?" I always know the answer to the question, to the best of my ability, by doing my research on the information that's out there. I also often ask detailed questions based on the research that I know the answer to and see if they know it, all the time reading their body language. The best is when you ask a pretty simple, basic question and no one can answer it. This is a great place to be.

Also find out what has kept the company from achieving or not achieving their goals, and what's impacted their performance during these times. You must know how they measure success. When I hear people talk about percentages, much like my 97% number, most of it is a WAG (Wild Ass Guess). I love that people think because they put something into a spreadsheet or Power Point presentation it's impactful and true. Numbers can be interpreted any way you want. If someone displays a line graph showing a 32% growth rate over last year, I can take the same numbers and by the magic of pretty pictures show how over the last year 68% of their business showed no growth, was stagnant and didn't improve. There are always two different ways to look at it, half full or half empty. Typically, middle management always wants to show it half full and salespeople always come in half empty so they can show them how to improve. However, you run the strong risk as a salesperson that you will make the person who is responsible for these numbers look bad if they buy from you. If you come in and show them how you can save them $15 million, what do you think their boss will think when they bring it to him? One of two things: "He's a good employee and is working hard to uncover more efficient ways to reduce costs," or (more than likely) Option 2, "Why are we identifying this savings only now, and why haven't you done so before in the last five years you've been here?" Be careful with the savings model, just because you can show tremendous savings doesn't mean you close it every time, you could be giving the person a black eye by exposing him.

After I have done all of my reading of annual reports and financial updates, I read the introductory information about the company, Chairman's Letter, etc. You will also want to listen to or dial into the prospect's quarterly review meetings when the CEO and CFO outline how they did. These can be pretty dry, but can also give you great information to get an appointment. Executives get a majority of their pay in stock, so presenting to potential investors and market analysts is a big deal for them. They spend weeks going over the information and their presentations. If you spend the time listening carefully to them speak, you can pull a story or phrase they use and leverage this as an approach to get a meeting with them. We'll discuss this approach in the next chapter.

Here's my bonus tip of the week: when doing your research on a company, call your stockbroker and tell them you are thinking of investing in that company. Let the stockbroker go and pull all the information on this company for you. Mine does a competitive market analysis of competitors in their space; it's pretty much butter. Oh and he's not getting a copy of this book, sorry Mark. You will have to invest once and awhile to keep this door open, though. This tip gives you insight as if you were an investor in the company, and some reservations you may have in investing your liquid cash could be some of the challenges the company is trying to overcome. Think about it, it's sort of a stock tip, right?

Map It Out

One great trick I do is once I have done all of my research, printed out who the executives are, what their goals and initiatives are (you have to listen to calls and read to find this out,) I sit. What I mean by this is that I try to understand what they do as a business, looking at it from the inside out. You have to envision yourself as the CEO of this company now that you have seen all the numbers and done your research. What would you do to leverage more revenue into this company?

I have a huge 6'x6' white board in my office at home. At the top of the board I write the company name and its vision statement or mission statement. Then I map out all of the key executives, CEO, CFO, and CIO, list the board members, etc. I create an organizational chart based upon my research. Note: you can always call into a company and ask the assistants whom they report to or who reports to them, if you do it the right way. Once I have the org chart up, I add what affects each person, as outlined during the last call. One I just did was for a CFO and his challenge was a 20% debt-to-capital ratio, and a 1% change in service revenue had a 90% basis change in gross margin. The CEO spoke about revenue and earnings per share and how the dividend yield was 2%. This is all great information to map out next to their name, or better yet, a picture of them on your org chart.

Here's my second tip of the week and this one is gold, this should pay for the cost of this book if you get nothing else out of it. I map the members of the Board of Directors on their own org chart board. By doing this I also map where they hold executive and non-executive positions within other companies. What you will find is that most sit on numerous boards for other companies. Then I expand my prospect list to include those companies and board members, and further map their board members out as well. You'll find it's this weird six degrees of separation between all of them in the Fortune 500 space, and yes, I can trace them all back to Kevin Bacon. Doing this allows me to also map the board members and what their role on the board is, Audit Committee, Executive Committee, Strategic Planning Committee, Governance & Nominating Committee, etc. If you do this the right way you will be amazed at what you discover.

I then look to see who the Mark is. The Mark, to me, is the ultimate approver of what I am selling. In my space it is usually the CFO or the person who reports directly to the CFO. I map all of this out to figure out whom I'm going to penetrate and try to speak to, and who is on the list below them in case I get pushed down and need to elevate myself back up. Be aware that this is a living and breathing process so it can change without notice.

I did this recently for an account where a new CFO (Tom) was appointed. He had been the treasurer for the company. The person who had the CFO position beforehand (Keith) was moved to an EVP position. Doing my research, I had mapped Tom, the new CFO, as my Mark and thought, "Perfect timing! He's going to be new and will want to make his own mark as CFO, and I'll show him how to do it." However, I was on their Q3 earnings call and the new CFO was a straight up prick. He was very abrasive and let the whole C-Level thing go to his head. You'll no doubt encounter some of these guys, they forget they put their pants on the same way you do, but hey, that's life. During the call when one of the analysts had a hard question for Tom to answer, the CEO deflected it to the former CFO (Keith). After Keith had answered the question the CEO let everyone on the call know that Tom reports to Keith and Keith reports to the CEO. So instantly my Mark changed from Tom to Keith. It can happen that quickly. How much time do you think I saved by identifying the true decision maker in this process first? If I hadn't been on that two-hour call I would have never known.

This is an example of why preparation is key. You're only going to get one shot at making a first impression, so make it your best. When you do your research and know what you're talking about I have found that most executives will respond even if they don't want to meet, or will push you down to someone who will listen. It's not unusual or uncommon for me to spend two to three weeks just doing research on a large organization prior to making a call in to them. But I'm also calling on the chickens as well, remember?

Research, research, research is crucial. It can only help you. Just make sure it's accurate and don't ever assume. If you're not sure about certain numbers get clarification prior to making any assumptions. I'm not sure if it's urban legend, but I've heard the horror story of the sales rep that did a presentation to the CFO and misread their earnings statement. Prior to showing him his solution pricing he had a slide which had a blanket statement he interpreted from their balance sheet. It was wrong, and the CFO corrected him. Bad salespeople will say, "That's no big deal," and move on. Think about this, the minute you have one piece of wrong data then all of your data is perceived as wrong data. This is why it is extremely important to have a validation meeting in your sales cycle. In the next several chapters I will discuss the steps or foundation I have put in place for my own personal sales cycle. My typical sales cycle consists of research, qualifying, discovery, bridge the gap, 1st appointment, bridge the gap again, 2nd appointment, validation meeting, pricing, bridge the gap and closing. Obviously no two sales are the same, but this is the foundation I try to follow when getting a close.

6 Letters, Emails, Phone Calls, Oh My!

Now that we are done with the appetizer we are going to jump right into the main course. I've noticed while writing this I've been on a diet so food seems to pop into my head more often than usual. I'd like to talk about how I structure my letters, emails and phone calls for account penetration. I'm going to show you how I get into Fortune 500 accounts at the CEO or CFO level for a conceptual meeting about my company and what I sell. As I've stated, this may or may not work for you, it all depends on the situation. There is no magic wand I wave that will allow you to have a 100% success rate, but I'm confident in this approach because it has worked for me time and time again. It's pretty amazing when you can pull out a name from a billion dollar company, have no relationship with the account whatsoever, yet with proper research get an audience with the CEO and CFO. Granted not all of my meetings are great and I don't close every one, but I do get in. Getting in is the main thing. I always say, if I can just get in to speak to them for five minutes then it's mine to lose. All I need is the shot or chance to tell my story.

The Cold Call

Prospecting or cold calling is one of the hardest things to do in sales and I hate it. I used to have sales managers who told me they loved it. Really? They must have some sick fix for rejection. I love the chase and challenge, but not the action of doing it. Maybe I'm a breed by myself when I say that, but it is what it is. I'm not like my old managers who thought it was a good use of time to go cold call by knocking on forty building doors in a day. I always thought this was a waste of time, and it showed you didn't value your prospect's time or care about them outside of just another number on the cold calling or business card collection sheet. If you're still being tracked by how many business cards you collect in a day, ouch! Get out as soon as possible. You don't want to be selling anything that requires that, trust me.

This is one area I truly appreciate about salespeople, even the bad ones. It's hard going in front of people out of the clear blue and making your case to meet them. You can tell when salespeople aren't at their number, their style changes to more of a begging to meet so that their manager can attend while in town shadowing. This is a prime example of how you're selling against numbers and strategy. There is no strategy to this sale, it's just contacting as many people as you can. For example, you make one hundred cold calls and set ten appointments, then out of those ten appointments three let you get to the next step. Out of those three appointments you close one of them. To me these numbers are a real waste of time. I agree that activity breeds results, but I also believe that the right and smart activity drives your close ratio way up. I'd rather meet ten truly qualified prospects in order to have the chance to close all ten. The difference is that I will take the time to qualify and do my research to find the right ten rather than blindly running door to door knocking. Also, I utilize the phone; I can reach more people that way than by knocking on doors.

My first job with Mr. D was in inside sales, selling telecommunication services to businesses. The turnover rate for this inside sales position had to be at least 90% every 90 days, it was pretty ridiculous. The business model was to get salespeople to make 120 phone calls a day, and whatever stuck out of those calls, stuck. If you weren't at your quota at the end of the month you didn't come back the next month. Looking back now, it was probably the best first sales job for me to have. It taught me how not to be afraid on the phone, taught me a strong work ethic in sales and showed me the ugly side of sales in general.

In this sales position if you were able to achieve your quota for five consecutive months then they would move you into outside sales. Luckily I achieved my five-month quota and moved to outside sales, bringing Mr. D with me as my manager since my numbers were the biggest anyone in the company had ever made. How did I do this? Simple, I called everywhere in the United States. When the other 30-40 sales reps punched out at 5:00PM Eastern Time I stayed until 8:00PM Eastern Time calling California. Every month no one understood how I was able to produce more. It was simple; more calls equaled more sales in this type of sales cycle. By staying later than the rest of the salespeople I was able to differentiate myself even in this area of sales.

Leads

Mr. D also helped me understand the reality of sales in a life lesson he taught me my first week on the job. I was in my cube young and dumb right out of college, trying to dial for dollars. I was making over 100 calls a day and I'm sure all of them were brutal, getting my teeth kicked in during the first week. On my fourth day on the job one of my cube-mates came out and said he had a great lead. Man was I dumb, I asked him, "Where do you get these leads you speak of?" To me it was this magical item or golden ticket someone had been keeping from me; a list of people who wanted to buy and all I had to do was call them to sign them up. I thought, "Wow! How do I get these?" He told me to go see Mr. D, and that he had the leads for me. I was flabbergasted, here I'd been calling and getting my butt kicked trying to get people to buy something from me while Mr. D had these "leads" all along!

I walked down the long row of people with headsets on and came to Mr. D's office. The door was open so I knocked and walked in. Now just so everyone knows, Mr. D is a large man, about 350 lbs., a big, big guy who used to play professional football for the Arizona Cardinals as an offensive lineman. This should give you some sort of visual. Mr. D was leaning back in his tiny chair behind his desk eating a sub sandwich, wearing much of it on his shirt. His large body formed a perfect tabletop right at chest level. I said to him, "Mr. D do you have leads I can get?" With a mouthful of food, Mr. D looked at me and said, "You want leads?" I said, "Yes, do you have some?" "Close my door," said Mr. D.

I turned around and closed his door then sat down in the chair in front of his desk. With another mouthful of food he said, "So you want leads huh?" I again asked, "Do you have them?" and Mr. D said "Yeah I have leads." I felt so relieved, and even began to chuckle and tell him about how I'd been getting my butt kicked making calls, and that I wouldn't be doing that if I'd had the leads he had. Mr. D said, "Oh, I'm sorry, I have your leads right here, you should have told me you wanted leads." Again I began to chuckle like it was some terrible miscommunication he and I had when I first got hired four days ago. He bent down behind his desk to retrieve the leads for me, still holding his sub and chewing the whole time. He was multi-tasking lunch, our conversation, and getting me my "leads." As he bent down to retrieve them from behind his desk I had enough time to have some fantasies race through my head: me in a nice car, holding fists of money, outside my mansion; all things young dumb salespeople think of.

Mr. D slowly rose from behind his desk with the leads, and the closer his arm came to the top of the desk the more excited I began to get. I anticipated the mother load of all leads. His arm came up and a large thump hit his desk. It was a huge Yellow Book phone book. Mr. D said, "Here's your leads, if I was you, I would start with R."

At that moment I learned an important life lesson: no one is going to help you in sales except yourself. Mr. D showed me there are no "leads" and every business out there is a lead, you just have to pick up the phone and find them. What a great lesson to learn just starting out as a salesperson. I was fortunate enough to have this strong foundation of coming up through the ranks of sales to what I'm doing now in a more strategic solution-based sales approach, but I still use that hardworking, make it happen approach.

IDENTIFYING THE MARK

I understand how tough it can be to penetrate accounts, and this is why I've elected to show you another way, my way, so take it for what it's worth. To penetrate an account there are several different approaches you can take and some of them you can take at the same time. I'm not going to give out all of my secrets or show you all of them in detail, but what I will do is lay the foundation so you can add to it with your own style and see if it works for you as it has for me.

When first penetrating a prospect that doesn't know me from Adam, I do the research I discussed in the last chapter. I map the account out on my white board, complete my org chart, and most importantly I identify my Mark. The Mark does not always have to be at the C-Level, he or she can be a couple of levels down, but I always like to start high knowing where I want to end up. So prior to even making a call or writing the letter, I identify whom I want to get a meeting with. What is the ultimate goal here? I love when I ask salespeople this and they say, "To get the appointment." Yeah, but with whom, specifically? Do you know his/her name? This is what you need to know so when you start getting passed around within the prospect's organization you know where you ultimately want to end up. Don't end up at the wrong level. Time management, remember?

Once I have the Mark identified, I circle them on my board. This is the person I want to meet with or have a conversation with. Next, in a different color marker I start to circle people on the org chart around my Mark who could influence my Mark. Then in a third color marker I circle people who could generate buzz about my company and me within their organization.

Here's an example. Let's say my Mark is identified as the SVP of Finance. This is the person with whom I want to have a conversation or meeting. I next map out who is above, below and lateral to him in the organization. Above him I want to map it all the way to the executive wing. Below him I only go one level down. Lower than that and you are going to have a long sales cycle and harder time climbing up the mountain to meet with them. Once all the players are identified I write a letter to each person. For this example, I would be writing a letter to the CEO, CFO, EVP Operations, SVP Finance (the Mark), VP Finance, Board of Directors and SVP of Corporate Services. This makes a total of fifteen letters, including one to each board member.

Letters

Every salesperson structures their letters the following way:

- Hi my name is so and so, I'd like to introduce myself.
- I do/my company does business with XYZ companies
- I'd like to meet with you

These are the building blocks for failure. It's important to tailor each letter towards the individual person and how it affects their business unit. **Each letter should be different and each one should talk about THEM throughout the entire letter.** If you look at the structure of most letters they only talk about me, me, and me. Grab the last letter you sent out and see how much it talks about the prospect, maybe one line or quote if you're lucky.

This is when all the hard work and research you have done pay off. **When you craft an intelligent letter using *their* terminology and show that you have done your research on them, you separate yourself from the hundreds of bad letters they receive every week from the other 97% of salespeople.**

Here's the opening of an actual letter written by a new salesperson who bought into my concept and system. It was sent to the CFO of a company, and yes, it got the appointment with him. One of the first things he said was how well-written and thought out the letter was.

> Dear Mr. Richardson,
> You expressed in your Annual Report for 2010 that the year had been difficult for your 2,400+ property portfolio as **only 4% of your total square footage was effectively reduced despite revenue being down 8% and staff numbers being down 12.3%, which made your square footage per head go up from 218 sq ft in 2008 to 230 sq ft in 2009.**

> **Over the next three years you plan to achieve a 7% cost-to-revenue ratio.** In order to achieve this you need to be able to **leverage centralized expertise and resources** so that **global strategies** can be applied on an **enterprise wide scale.**

Look at the structure of this letter compared to the first example of how most salespeople write their letters. There is no "me" in the letter, no introduction, etc. Always talk about them. What is important to them? What affects their organization? Right away your letting him know you've done your research and you understand what challenges he is facing. You must tailor it around what you know you can sell him, which is very important. Don't quote or talk about things you can't directly affect.

What do you think the next paragraph is about? Me or my company? Nope, it talks about averages with my customers and how his target of 7% is half of what my average customer is doing with 15%. **You need to show that you are the expert, and get them to think, "I need to meet with him, maybe he knows something I don't."**

This is the art of selling; convincing them that you're different then everyone else and that you can help them. I tailor most of my letters towards what is hot for that particular individual. For the CEO, I structured the letter to focus on their acquisition model and how this expansion will play out in the next two years with their strategy. The key is to differentiate yourself from the pack. Talk about them and not you. How can you help their problem or help them better serve their customers?

In most of my letters to executives I do request a meeting; however, I do not request to speak to them in order to set the meeting up. I let them know I will contact their assistant (put their assistant's name in the letter, remember research!) This is key; most executives do not know their own schedule, they have trusted assistants who keep them to their schedules and meetings. Don't be that guy who always tries to plow through the receptionist. What most salespeople don't realize is that in many instances the executive assistants in the Fortune 500 space have been with their boss for ten to twenty years. Leverage them; they can be your best friends for getting a meeting. You can turn them from a gatekeeper to a gate opener.

When I send letters to board members and executives I also always send copies to their assistants, in which I introduce myself and let them know I'll be following up with them in the next day or two. I let them know I don't need to speak to the executive directly as my letter states. This has worked well for me. The assistants like that you have given them the professional courtesy of informing them and you have also given them some control by scheduling the appointment, they eat this up as well.

The reason I never want to talk to the executive on the phone is selfish on my part, I like talking to them in person better. If the CFO picks up the phone, he is going to try to figure out where to push me down to as quickly as possible, or disqualify me altogether. I like speaking in person so I can read body language, facial expressions and get a gut reading on the person. It's just personal preference, but I feel it also values his time rather than trying to immediately get him out of his day to talk about what I am selling, which is what most salespeople do.

In the last paragraph of my letters I write that I won't need to speak to them personally when I call in the next day or two. All they have to do is let (and I use their assistants' name in the letter) know of some dates when they would be able to meet for 15 minutes face to face. I never ask for anything outside of 15 minutes. You are looking for a conceptual meeting. It's kind of like when you're dating, you know within the first 15 minutes of the date if it's going anywhere. Executives do, too. If you ask for a meeting for an hour, you'll never get it.

Here's another golden nugget I'll share which has had an almost 85% success rate for me (remember what I said about stats): board member letters. This is an approach I've used which often works. If my book takes off this could change, but in the meantime this trick is yours to keep. When I've done my research and mapped out the Board of Directors and where they serve outside of the company I'm trying to penetrate, I send letters to where they are active, but to the attention of the company on whose board they sit. For example, I want to penetrate ABC Company. One of the board members (Mike) for ABC Company is the CEO for XYZ Company. I send a letter to Mike at XYZ Company with reference to or attention ABC Company. **HE OPENS IT EVERY TIME!** No other salesperson is doing this type of research, and he opens it every time because he never gets mail addressed to him as a board member outside of the company itself. Yes, it is a thing of beauty and it has worked amazing for me; a nugget I have kept quiet all this time. I can't tell you how many times I have received direct communication from the board member via email, phone, etc. Most board members cannot make the decision to help me with the sale, but they sure can point me in the right direction and have tremendous clout in helping to secure appointments. The other added beauty is that now you're communicating with another executive who is probably the decision maker at another top account you can penetrate. It's like a 2 for 1 sale and you have coupons!!

The key with letters is to differentiate yourself and get the buzz going around in the organization. The more your letter gets passed around, the better your chances of securing an appointment. Another great trick I do is to put in my letter that I have reached out and sent a letter to _____ (and here I list every person's name I'm sending letters to.) This works well because people don't like when you reach out to the Board of Directors, especially the C-Suite, so they usually contact me to see what it's about.

I had one CEO from a Fortune 100 company send an email to me based on my letter, and he copied all of the members of the Board of Directors on the email. He stated that they were good where they were at and that he appreciated my letter. I called him out on the numbers he was not achieving (go to the video tape, the numbers don't lie.) His response was a preventative one where he tried to disqualify me and my letter, and he gave a nice self-promotion plug in the email about how all of his goals were being met. One of the board members bounced off the email to him and me directly and asked for the letter. I gave the CEO about three hours to respond, and when he didn't I forwarded the letter to the board member and copied the CEO. The next day the CEO's assistant called and wanted to grant me the meeting with the CEO. This is a great example of how a board member can help facilitate a meeting.

Another great trick with board members is with all the information out there today you can typically find their home addresses; some of their mail via the company is sent there. I got one of my biggest meetings with an executive in the Fortune 5 space by sending my letter to a board member's house via FedEx the Thursday before Christmas. I don't recommend doing this every time, but it was a last ditch effort to gain a meeting in the account after several approaches hadn't worked. I was lucky this one worked, but I haven't done it enough to know the success rate. However it's something to think about as well.

Emails

I'm not a fan of sending out email blasts to people, this seems like something Marketing came up with and you know how I love Marketing. Spamming people just shows exactly what I'm preaching against, it shows no effort or research. The old school sales approach throws everything up against the wall and sees what sticks. This probably yields about the same results as direct mailings, about 1%. So you can do the math to see if it's worth your time. There are some people who say, "All you need is one." Keep playing the lottery, "All you need is one" to win that as well.

I use email to communicate meeting schedules and appointments. I rarely will communicate value adds or solutions via email, that's just asking for trouble. **Never, ever send pricing via email**. I see this all the time and it never pans out, but salespeople still do it. They will be working with a prospect for some time, they've met them face-to-face, etc. Somehow in the sales process the pricing portion comes up, and the prospect tells them "Send me your pricing" or "Email me you're pricing." Without hesitation most salespeople fire it off to them and then end the email with something stupid like, "Call me if you want to discuss," or "Give me a call so we can schedule a time to review it." This always cracks me up. How often has that worked out? Ask yourself, why the urgency for the pricing in the sales process and why now? Most of the time you don't know the answer, so you shouldn't be sending the pricing.

Here's what typically happens. A bad salesperson is engaged with the prospect, meets with them a couple of times, has them forecasted, and thinks everything is great and moving forward. The prospect asks for pricing, and the sales rep sends over the pricing with the ridiculous comments at the end of it. Then: no movement. The bad salesperson calls and leaves ridiculous messages such as, "Just checking in to see if you got it," "Wanted to make sure you didn't have any questions," or "Wanted to know if you needed anything else." Come on, really? What has happened is that salesperson has instantly turned into the 97%, and has become the annoying salesman checking in or trying to get an "update" on where things are.

Grab your balls and control the sales process. You've taken what has been a pleasurable experience from the beginning and changed it into Mr. Annoying Sales Guy looking for his order and wondering how it went cold. It went cold because chances are you shouldn't have sent them the pricing in the first place, you didn't know where they were in their buying process or decision process. Much like throwing up and product selling, you just sent it blindly. Make sure you always have them on the phone to review pricing or do a WebEx to review it.

Once you give pricing or your proposals out you have lost control of the sale, it's that simple. Think about the last time you bought some big-ticket item, like a car. Didn't you shop the competition? Didn't you ultimately wait to see what their pricing was so you could compare it to others you were looking at? Didn't you notice what was really important to you in the quote and how some salespeople missed it and some got it? Your prospects are doing the same to you. Don't you even want to validate the numbers with the customer prior to sending it out? This goes back to qualifying in your first appointment what they have in terms of budget and time frames for change. Keep in mind that I'm not talking about RFP responses here. If you're responding to an RFP then you have accepted the company policies and procedures so when they say send pricing, you send pricing. I'll talk more about pricing in Chapter 11.

Phone Calls

I hold phone calls dear to my heart since this is how I made my first impression on the sales world, dialing for dollars. Phone calls that follow up on the letters you just mailed are key to the success of your letters. The research time and effort you put into the letters mean nothing if you can't have similar results via the phone. When following up on the letters we discussed earlier, be sure you have the letter in front of you, just in case.

You always want to make your first call to the Mark, the person you have identified as the one you want to meet. This call will dictate whether you have to go above or below them for a different approach into the account. I typically call the assistant as I mentioned in the letter and my structure is pretty much the same. You can tweak it or change it to whatever fits you best, but this is typically what I say: "I'm following up on a letter which was mailed on ABC Date and should have arrived in your office on XYZ Date (If overnighted you can see when and who signed for it). Did Jim get the letter?" Let her answer this question, but don't go down the rabbit hole she may try to lead you into with "What is it about," or "What is it in reference to?" If she asks this, I sometimes say, "The same letter was also sent to David Waters, Mark Booya, Steve Ohoh," (I list the other people in the organization I sent the letter to: CEO, Board members, etc.) All you're trying to find out is if they have seen the letter. If they have not seen or read the letter then get a time from her when she thinks they will have read it by, and let her know you will now be contacting (say all the names again of the people to whom you mailed the letter) as outlined in the letter. Please make sure you tell the assistant you do not need to speak with their boss personally.

Here's where we find out if you've been paying attention. Earlier I told you I always send their assistants copies of each individual letter so they have it for their records, along with an introduction letter from me to the assistant. If you've remembered and done this step you won't have as "cold" a script as I just outlined for you. Just checking to making sure you're getting it.

If the Mark has seen the letter and is not interested, ask if he has sent it down to anyone else in the organization. This is a key step which you can leverage well when you've done it often enough. If the assistant says the CFO did read it and passed it along to someone else (for example, to Steve, Director of Facilities), here's a tip which works really well. Whomever they have passed it down to, have the assistant who told you this information transfer you to that person's assistant if they have one, or to them directly. When you get good enough and are able to build rapport well, you can ask her not only to transfer you, but to please introduce you to them as well. This works like butter. If it's another assistant, they all know each other and it's an easy layup for an appointment. If it's to Steve directly and he does not have an assistant, it's still an easy layup because you have the CFO's assistant basically asking him to meet with you.

When you get really good you can ask the CFO's assistant, "I appreciate Jim allowing me to speak with someone in the organization. Just so I understand your internal process better, with whom would I meet **BEFORE** it would come to Jim's desk?" I don't know why but for some reason when you use the word "before" it works. Here's where things can get treacherous, so pay attention. If she gives you the name of the person who typically handles everything before it gets in front of the CFO, you're butter. Thank her for all of her help and let her know you will meet with Steve to see if there is enough interest to bring it in front of the CFO.

While you have her on the phone, you can also ask her if she would mind penciling you in for a meeting with the CFO three or four months out just in case the meeting with the contact she provided is interested in moving ahead. Let her know that if there is no interest you will call back and she can take it off her calendar. Get this date if you can. Since it's so far out and you're asking her to pencil it in, assistants will typically do this. They figure there's plenty of time to cancel it or you'll call back and take it off the schedule. And don't forget, have her transfer you and introduce you to Steve, the push-down.

When I get on the phone with the push-down or even meet them face to face I let them know I have a meeting scheduled with the CFO on the date I just set with the assistant. I also let them know that it's dependent upon their level of engagement with me. I tell them that before I meet with the CFO I want to meet with them. This works wonders, and you can steer this push-down to come up with ideas you can share with the CFO. I'll typically say something like, "I want to work with you and include you in on this meeting with the CFO."

Then I have Steve or his assistant call the CFO's assistant. You've just confirmed an appointment with the decision maker for your sale and the business owner. Be careful, you have to do this the correct way, and it has to be done ethically. Don't try this approach your first time, it's like a fine wine, you have to let it sit for a while. Start with the basic foundation I have outlined and then expand upon that based upon your prospects and your type of sales/industry.

Once I have a meeting scheduled, I send an agenda. **Always send the agenda to the assistant prior to the meeting.** Keep it very professional with bullet points, 2 or 3 topics only. Have them add to it and get input if possible. Assistants will rarely give you input if the C-Level has even seen it, but it gives them something to print out and hand to the prospect ten minutes before you walk into the meeting. I hear salespeople always say they don't like doing this because it gives the prospect an opportunity to cancel. Really? Then it's not much of a prospect is it? Why would I waste my time and company resources to find that out in person? I'd much rather they tell me now than have me fly out there, meet with them and get the same result. A trick to keep ahead of the game on this is to send the assistants your travel itinerary. Let them see your flight, hotel, car rental, etc. Once you have confirmed all of this and they see you're traveling from out of town they will be less likely to cancel. This is another example of giving them some control so they work for you in the long run.

It is important to realize that even the best approaches using letters, phone calls and emails could net you zero results. Sales is also about timing. I've had plenty of examples I can share where my letter and penetration into the account was great, but the timing was wrong. You'll see this when they start pushing you towards meeting with some of the consultants they've hired, which is pretty typical.

I've been successful and continue to be because I understand that in order to achieve these high level meetings you need to differentiate yourself from everyone else. I'm not talking about cheesy gimmicks or anything like that, just showing you have earned the right to speak with them and you are the subject matter expert in your field. Have you ever thought of writing a letter to an organization listing the challenges they're more than likely facing around what you are selling? Chances are good that they have no idea about your solution and have never even looked at it before.

The real art of selling is not when you're presenting, it's finding out from the prospect why they elected to meet with you in the first place. For whatever reason, they will never come out and tell you, "this is what we are challenged with, this is what we are looking for." They hold this information close to their chest. This is what you have to figure out; why did they grant me this meeting? What in my talk track, letter, email, etc., grabbed their attention and touched on some issue they are facing now? Once you can identify this, then you have uncovered the true opportunity.

7

Bridging the Gap

As we discussed earlier, sales typically go cold because you're missing something, didn't qualify it properly or had bad luck, right? One thing I do in any engagement is a next step. *Next step* means an agreed upon date/time confirmed by the prospect. It's an actual date and time, not something vague like "next week" or "Thursday." This seems simple and obvious but it's still easy for me to forget even to this day. In every meeting I attend, I have my call guide and in the last section the last thing I write every time is NEXT STEP. This is critical to keeping the momentum of your sale moving forward; strike while the iron is hot. If you are not controlling the sales cycle then the prospect is, and they tend to want to move slowly. In sales, much like in sports, speed kills. You have to move quickly in sales in order for all the moving parts to be aligned toward a *yes* decision.

How often have you given a presentation or a WebEx and the person tells you they need to meet internally to discuss and review it as a team? This happens all the time. How often do you get a set time/date after they tell you this? Probably rarely, if ever. Bad salespeople say, "Okay" and get off the phone or leave the meeting. Good salespeople accept "Call me next week." Great salespeople ask, "What decision making process do you have to go through internally and what will change between now and next week?" These types of questions may seem awkward at the time, especially the first time you ask them, but they are necessary. If you don't qualify a next step, then much like when you email pricing, you turn into that annoying sales guy "Just checking in," or "Seeing if you made a decision." I've gotten to the point where I'll tell my prospect, "Just so we all have the same expectations and I don't turn into the annoying sales guy, 'just checking in for updates,' what is a set date and time we can talk?" You will be amazed at how much this will shorten your sales cycle and rescue it from Limbo-land.

If it's hot enough for them to meet internally and review, yet they can't pin down a date for you, you should question how hot it really is in their minds. If people want to do business with you and are engaging you to do business then why should it be hard for you to ask these questions? Most salespeople don't ask these questions because they're afraid of the answer and want to live in Lala-land in regards to how they think the deal is going. They're hoping the prospect walks them down the sales process favoring the salesperson, rather than walking the prospect down their sales process with an action to close.

Whenever I talk to my sales counterparts about a deal and they utter the phrase "I think" in any sentence about their prospects, I give them a 20% chance of getting the sale. If you're guessing what your prospect is thinking you are not on the same page as your prospect, even just in strategy alone. Now add to that the decision process, pricing, implementation, contracts, etc. You can quickly get off target with your prospect unless communication is open between the two of you. If I'm working with a prospect and they make the communication piece a one-way street, or if they only share what they feel is necessary for me to know, in most cases I will walk away from the opportunity. If you don't have mutual communication to do business then you're wasting your time. My time is valuable, I'm aware of this, and I show my prospects that theirs is just as important as mine.

The moral of the story is to do a "Bridge the Gap" call. Get on the phone with your prospect prior to any conference call, face-to-face meeting, WebEx or video conference. The purpose of bridge the gap calls are exactly that, they bridge any gaps that may have come up between the last meeting you had and the next one coming up. Have you ever had a great meeting, and then at the next one the first thing the prospect does is tell you how everything has completely changed? Now your presentation doesn't really have any value. The purpose of the bridge the gap call is to help move all of your prospects towards the goal of *sold*.

One of the first things to ask in a bridge the gap call is, "Since the last time we spoke, has anything changed?" (This is also good to do at any second appointment meeting.) Next you want to go over all of the hot topics in your first meeting or conversation. List their challenges and how they measure success. Make them tell you exactly what this is in their minds. If you don't get this information, your sale is in jeopardy.

One red flag to look for when doing these calls is if your prospect starts switching what they say their challenges are from meeting to meeting. A textbook example of this and how it happens all the time is when they keep telling you different things they want to see. Last meeting they told you they wanted to see about consolidating databases and the integration piece. During the bridge the gap call, they don't bring any of that up, but instead talk about dashboards and reporting capabilities. Red Flag!! Call them out on it, this is obviously a miscommunication between the two of you so don't feel awkward for one second for calling them out on it. Chances are they are shopping you or are not the true decision makers in this process, no matter what their title or what they tell you.

Bridge the gap calls are also great for identifying the key players at the prospect's company. It's essential to identify who your players are and what their roles are. Every large deal has the following players:

- Approver
- Decision Maker
- Problem Owner
- Influencer
- Coach
- Champion
- Saboteur

If you don't have all these identified in the big accounts you're working now, you should try and figure them out. Like in the board game Clue, these are the same players in every large deal, they are the usual suspects with the usual titles. Not only do you have to identify which person fits each role, you must also understand their role and position as it relates to your sale. You have to know what each person can gain by buying from you, and what their criteria is for selecting you. How are they involved in the decision process and what is their level of influence in this decision? Most importantly, where are they in their buying cycle? Do they think they need what you're selling right now? The higher up you get the more important this information is. Timing is everything in sales, sometimes you get the right person at the right time and it's great. Sometimes you have the right person, but the timing is wrong. Most commonly you have the wrong person and the timing is wrong as well, you got involved too late in the process.

In terms of the large complex deals I'm selling, here's what each of these roles means to me:

Approver – This may be the person you never meet. It may not be the signature on your contract, but it's someone who looks over everything and gives his blessing prior to it being signed. (High Level)

Decision Maker- This is the person who will sign your contract or has budgetary control over your sale and what it is affecting.

Problem Owner- This is the person who feels the day to day challenges

Influencer – Someone who could persuade the decision maker or other members of the organization to be either in favor of or against your sale.

Coach – Someone who is giving you tips or helping you in the account to understand their internal processes or what their boss would want to see. Be careful, coaches can be coaches to your competition as well.

Champion- This is the person who has something personal to gain with your sale. For example, you saving their company money gets them their bonus or they get promoted, so they put their necks out on the line for you and your company.

Saboteur- This is the person who is against what you're selling. Your sale makes them look bad or discredits something they created, built, bought or implemented. These are going to be the most defensive people in your meetings.

Knowing all of these different roles is important, and you can figure many of these roles out while performing the bridge the gap calls. Just look at who attends. As a salesperson, knowledge is key, and when you don't know something about the political landscape of your prospect you can get into trouble, lose the sale very quickly, and not even know it until it's too late.

During your bridge the gap call, go through the DK and DK^2 approach with your prospects; if you're not sure about something label it a DK (Don't Know.) If you're not sure because you haven't asked the question, it's a DK^2 (Don't know what you don't know.) It's very important that you challenge yourself as a salesperson. I like to make a list of DK's and DK^2's after my first appointment but before my second appointment. Then these are the questions I ask on my bridge the gap call.

Prospects are more than happy to jump on a quick 15 minute call the day before you are scheduled to present. Remember, this has to be a good use of their time as well. Ask the questions you don't know the answers to during the bridge the gap call. If you have a coach or champion in the account, that's even better. In a committee environment I ask about the other members who will be at my presentation whom I haven't met yet. What is their role, to whom do they report? How did they get selected to this committee? You'll be amazed how much information you can get if your questions are well structured.

You must have these bridge the gap calls to keep the momentum moving and keep your deal moving towards the close stage. If your prospect will not get on these calls then you need to ask yourself if they are a true prospect and if you're really moving down to the close stage. Also, who's controlling the sales process?

8 First Appointment

You've secured the meeting with your prospect, now is the time to plan and create a strategy of how you are going to run the appointment. Here I'll be discussing how to conduct a face-to-face meeting. In order to be successful at your first appointment, you have to be well prepared and anticipate anything. You can enter the first appointment thinking one thing and then two minutes into the meeting you could have the strong realization that it's something else and you're not prepared to discuss it. The key is preparation and planning, but don't over think it because all the preparation and planning in the world can go out the window pretty quickly.

When preparing, you're going to want to have DK questions and clarification questions based upon your research. When I ask my sales colleagues what is the outcome you're looking to accomplish at this meeting, I typically get answers like, "To sell them," "Get another appointment," "Move to the next step," etc. These are all disasters waiting to happen. **The first appointment is for you to get a *yes* or *no*, and to get rid of the *maybes*.** Maybe's will kill any salesperson. You will end up spending too much time working it and working it, but it will rarely pan out to a *yes*.

My goal in a first appointment is to establish myself as an expert and convince them they need to look at what I'm showing them, my thought process. You typically want to position your questioning as open-ended questions, but also expand these. Ask the prospect challenging questions. Ask situational questions, cost and budget questions, needs questions and compelling reason-to-change questions. I lost an account one time, and when I did my Win/Loss report (see Chapter 13) with them after the fact the VP told me that I didn't give them a compelling reason to change. I know this is a blow-off answer, and now I ask this in my first meeting so I don't have to hear it ever again as an excuse. I ask them what would be their compelling reason to change; I let them tell me so later in the sales process I can bring it back up to them. I'm not going to get involved with all the different types of questions to ask, every opportunity is different. I will show you how to be prepared and what you should accomplish at the first appointment.

The first appointment should be all about them and less about you. You'll have your moment to pat you and your companies' capabilities on the back later in the sales process. The first appointment is meant to uncover the need for you to work with them now, not later, now. Urgency and a compelling reason for them to move forward with you is your takeaway from the first appointment. One thing I always find out in the first appointment even if I don't get the second appointment is what their internal decision process and budgetary approval process are. This may be different in your sale, but for me I have to uncover the answer to the question, "Are the necessary funds available for us to continue moving forward?" If the initiative is not budgeted for this year, do they have a discrepancy fund they can tap into? All of this needs to be uncovered in the first meeting to save time.

I worked with a young sales guy and he always felt uncomfortable asking about budget in the first meeting, he thought it was too premature. The difference between his mindset and mine was that I figured out after this meeting if it was worth pursuing and devoting my resources to it. He could spend three to four months meeting and working on it, with buy-in at the VP level, but at the end of the day it wasn't budgeted for this year. They would try to get it into the budget for the next year, and he'd end up involved in a long process to do this. Also, chances are he just made himself the baseline by which they will measure his competition and possibly go out to RFP.

By doing the proper research and getting the meeting face-to-face, you can uncover the thing which made them want to meet with you. The key is not to assume what that is, but to ask them what it is. One of the first things I will ask in my first appointment is what it was about the letter I sent them they liked, what got them interested enough to accept the appointment? They will generally tell you the pain they think you may be able to help alleviate.

You have to be able to show your value and how your company fits into any challenge they are facing. Don't jump right into the throwing-up syndrome; every bad salesperson does it. Think of the first appointment as *you* interviewing *them* to see if you want to do business with them. I know I can help every customer I meet with, the difference is, is it the right time to help them and do they think this as well. What you're selling will determine what information you need to get in the first appointment. You should be doing the least amount of talking as possible, let *them* throw up on *you*.

My sales require that we do an analysis of current state in order to provide a future state recommendation. Typically I have a couple of tricks to see how big of a stick my contact does or doesn't carry within their organization. If by the end of the meeting it has gone well and I'm convinced it will move forward, I will ask for each of us to sign a non-disclosure agreement (NDA.) By signing an NDA both parties can feel comfortable about the data being shared.

When I presented to an internet search firm that rhymes with Smoogle, I made them sign an NDA prior to our first meeting. It shows a level of interest in what we're going to be talking about. If they can't get an NDA signed or give you one of theirs, question what level you're contact is at in the account and how interested they are. Remember, we are there to do business, not meet people just to meet people. This brings up another quick point; the harder the appointment is to get with a person the better chance it is you are meeting with the right person. If they meet with you the first time you speak with them, you should wonder if they are meeting just to meet.

If your sale requires any type of analysis, whether you charge or do it for free, you can find out whom you're meeting with quickly with this tip. If your prospect has agreed to let you move forward and perform an analysis or review of their data, let them know you need a $0 Purchase Order in order to make it happen on your end. Two things here, first if they set you up in their internal system in order to issue a $0 Purchase Order you are set up in the system for future revenue. You have effectively gone around their Purchasing department requirements and its long drawn out process. Second, if the person you're meeting with does not have the authority to get you into their system for a $0.00 PO, do you think they will have the authority to sign off on $14 million? Doing this also shows the contact's interest in you and if they are going to be a partner. Your contact will have to get purchasing and finance involved to make this happen, and if he's unwilling to do this then how willing will he be to really look at your solution when you present?

Constantly challenge and qualify your opportunities so you don't waste your time. Let's say they agree to give you their numbers or data so you can look at it. The NDA is signed, PO is cut. At the end of the first appointment you have defined their internal approval process, identified key players, know their challenges, criteria for change, budgetary process and approval. Once you have all of this information you can move forward to the next step. Yes, before leaving you have to go over the action items on both ends (put dates with each one) and then get a solid next step date/time to come back for the second appointment. Many of the larger deals can have 100 calls, appointments, meetings, etc. and I get that. But here I'm just trying to show my high level sales foundation. You're ready for the next step.

9

VALIDATION MEETING

You've completed your first appointment and obtained agreement on moving to the second meeting with a set date and time. The prospect has provided you with their data so you can conduct an analysis to see how you can help improve their business. Most salespeople now have numbers they can show: cost savings or ROI. Think back to what I first talked about, ROI alone doesn't sell deals. I know a sales rep that showed a large software company a documented $150 million a year in savings and they still did not move forward with his solution. If you sell on price they'll leave you on price. Sell the vision, the dream, the concept, and let the ROI or savings be the cherry on top. **Most salespeople can't wait to get in front of the prospect and present their numbers. This is the biggest mistake I see happen in the sales cycle.** You have to do a validation meeting prior to presenting. This is a must, and you will see how much more positive your sales process turns out.

Bad salespeople spend much of the entire second appointment going over the numbers, typically in front of a group of people on the prospect's side. When you do this you leave yourself open, remember if one number or calculation is wrong then they are all wrong. You're inviting a buzz saw to come down on your deal. You're also setting yourself up for the prospect to tell you at the end of the meeting, "Let us review it and get back to you." Yep, you set yourself up for it before you even get to the meeting, so typical.

This is how I outclass my competition every day, and they wonder how I'm the thought leader with the customer. I have a validation meeting, and as always, face-to-face is best. This is what you should set at the end of your first appointment, not the second appointment or presentation, but the validation meeting. **The purpose of the validation meeting is to review the numbers they gave you and validate that they are accurate, especially if you had to make assumptions due to missing data**. If you haven't gotten anything from them, now's a great time to expose it. Tell them that you can't show them XYZ because you're still waiting on those numbers. You'll be amazed at how quickly you can get all the data when you do it this way.

The validation meeting is just that, a meeting to validate the numbers. You want them to agree that all the numbers they gave you are accurate. You don't have to show your numbers or solution in this meeting. This is not the purpose of the validation meeting, only to validate numbers and data or get missing information from them. They have to say, "Yes you are reading all the numbers correctly." This is especially important if you're taking yearly numbers and making them monthly. This method is so strong when applied correctly.

What is the first thing you ask at the start of the validation meeting? If you guessed, "Has anything changed since the last time we spoke?" then you are correct, winner-winner-chicken-dinner. When the prospect agrees that *their* numbers are correct then you won't be challenged on *your* numbers during your second appointment, since they will be based on the prospect's current validated numbers. This is even more important when you go down from the C-level to collect the data then back up to the C-level to present the data. You must have the people whom you collected the data or numbers from validate that they are accurate. This way if you're ever challenged in a meeting or presentation you can say, "These numbers are your numbers validated by Chris, Mark and Susan." It's strong and great for credibility.

Now that you've validated the numbers, in your second appointment you can talk about your solution rather than the numbers. I've presented before where I didn't even show the numbers because I had validated them beforehand. I was going against two competitors for the prospect. After my second appointment I was talking about implementation timeline and they were still reviewing numbers with the prospect. Who do you think won the account? The perception was that I was ahead of everyone else, and even though I might not have been, it was perceived that way. The prospect told me years later that this was one of the things that separated me from the competition, and the game changed to my favor by doing the validation meeting when no one else did. Small things like this differentiate you from the pack and can land you the deal; it can be that one extra step that no one else is doing which wins the deal.

Out for a beer one night with the same customer, he told that me by doing the validation meeting and presenting first for my second meeting I moved them along in the decision process faster. When he met the other two competitors for their second meeting after me, he felt like he had already seen their stuff a while back, and felt that they weren't moving forward but looking back instead. At the end of the second meeting the competitors fell into the bad habit of not even setting a next step, and they bought hook, line and sinker into, "Our team has to review it and we'll get back with you." Sound familiar? I already had the customer engaged in next steps on implementation and timelines for departmental roll out. Who controlled the sales process and who got controlled?

Okay, I'm off my soapbox now, let's move onto that second appointment.

10
Second Appointment

If you have done all the previous steps, or maybe just parts of them and then added your own individuality, that's great. If you have completed the validation meeting then you are at the point where your solution is the best thing since sliced bread and your prospect is going to save a ton of money. You're making your champion look like a rock star and all the moons and stars are aligned. Ok, back to reality.

The purpose of the second meeting is to really sell. Remember when I said be patient, you can talk about your capabilities later; this is later. This is the meeting where you have to show them that, as the expert, you know more about what's best for their organization than they do. This is why companies always outsource people, services, products, etc., they want to focus on what they're good at. For example, if you're a telecom salesperson calling on a healthcare company, keep in mind that they didn't get big because they know a lot about telecom. Just because the company you're dealing with may have employees or a department that has been in that particular field for some time doesn't mean the company is an expert. The cigarette manufacturer I referenced earlier outsources everything that does not directly relate to the making and packaging of cigarettes.

Keep all of this in mind when attending your second meeting. Remember that you have gotten this far down the sales process because you identified a challenge they are having and differentiated yourself from the 97%. The best advice I can give you, especially if you're selling to the C-Suite, is to equate your pricing to their metrics. C-Suite people generally look at specific areas or buckets when trying to run their organization as a whole. They are looking at things like **Revenue, SG&A, cash flow, asset efficiency, cost reduction, cost avoidance, cycle time, achieving strategy, company image, quality of services/product, sustainability and employee satisfaction**. This is what keeps them up at night, not your particular product, service or solution. The key is to take what you're selling and fit it into one of these buckets.

For example, before my second appointment meeting I try to list all the advantages of my sale. This is the "why go with you" portion. With all the research I've done I typically put together a strong four or five top reasons why they should select me. Here's the art of the sale on the complex side, but you can try it even with your smaller prospects to get the hang of it. Take the twelve areas I listed above. Now take the four advantages your sale has, try to put them into one of those twelve buckets, and explain how they fit in. For example, if you say that one of your four advantages is to improve turnaround time, how would improving turnaround time help revenue? How would improving turnaround time help SG&A? How would improving turnaround time help cash flow? So on and so forth.

You may not be able to show how some of your advantages can help in any of the buckets, and in this case you may want to reconsider if it's really an advantage your sale has over the competition or what they are currently doing in-house. For some of your advantages, you may be able to demonstrate how they help in a majority of the buckets, and this is great. **If you can demonstrate how an advantage affects a bucket, and if you can show a specific example and get the prospect to agree to what it would be worth to them monetarily, you will close every time.**

When you get really good you can start using this approach during your validation meetings. If you can have the prospect tell you how it affects these areas and put a value, or more importantly, a dollar amount to it then you are way ahead of the game. If you start to use this concept with success then you can even expand upon this and start having each problem owner agree to each buck individually, you will knock it out of the park.

Since all meetings are different and they depend upon the players and prospects, I won't go into how to specifically conduct the meeting. I will give you some tips that have helped me move along in the sales process. The second appointment should be about your proposal, and you should make the prospect understand your value. Don't forget, only give up your pricing and solution when you are sure that you're at the absolute last step in their buying process. One quick qualification I'll secure prior to presenting pricing is to have the contract sent to their legal department for the first round of red lines. What they do with the contract will demonstrate whether they want to allocate resources or if they're just shopping you and have managed to duck & hide during your prior qualification steps.

You should also find out what happens after they see your proposal. Seems simple, doesn't it? But how often do you blatantly ask your customer prior to presenting your solution, "Once we review the solution, if it meets all of your needs what are the next steps and the time frame around those steps?" Not that often, I'm sure. As salespeople we get so excited to show our solution we lose focus of the steps needed to get there, and also the steps needed to get beyond the presentation stage. If solution alone sold it then websites would be created for customers to input their data and buy the solution that gets kicked out. It just doesn't work that way. The art of selling is just that, an art.

By the second meeting you should know exactly where you stand in the account and what factors you need to overcome in order to secure your deal. If you have no idea where you stand then fall back. Do another bridge the gap call to figure it out, but the minute you don't know and you give up your solution you've lost control of the deal. Not only do you have to be wary of competitors, you also have to worry about your prospect looking to in-house your solution. This has happened to me more than once. At the end they have their IT departments try and create something or they leverage an existing system and try to do a customized module for it. Whatever the reason, it happens.

You also need to be aware of "happy ears" syndrome. It's when the prospect is telling you everything you want to hear and the sale seems like it's a slam dunk. Think about all the deals you've worked; doesn't it seem like the ones which felt like a layup were the ones you lost? And the ones you felt you messed up on are the ones you won? Maybe it's just me.

The second appointment can be positioned to be your best leverage in closing the prospect. Remember to validate their numbers prior to the second appointment so you can truly discuss your solution and the impact of your numbers. Again, try to have the prospect confirm how their numbers affect one of the twelve buckets the C-Suite is constantly looking at, and if they can put a dollar amount to it, even better. With this information you have set the foundation of your sales cycle and positioned yourself apart from your competition. You can now truly "sell" the prospect.

11

Pricing

We talked earlier about not emailing pricing to your prospect the minute they ask for it. So when *is* the right time to send pricing? Only when they're ready to buy, the last step in the sales process.

One of my vices is cars. I've loved cars ever since I was a little boy. I'm lucky if I can stay in a car two years before getting the itch to get another one. This means I go car shopping a lot, and I've dealt with tons of car salespeople. Here's a tip for buying a car: when I go car shopping I walk into the showroom and look for the sales board. I find the lowest guy on the sales board for the month and ask for him. I love peoples' expressions when I ask this, they're always amazed he has a customer in the lobby. So here comes this sales guy who hasn't sold anything all month, I look at him and say, "You need to sell some cars buddy and I'm here to buy one." I do it because I know he will bring whatever offer I give him to his manager. He will fight for me harder than the top guy because chances are he's out of a job at the end of the month.

My point with the car story is that people haven't been able to sell me on a car if I wasn't ready to buy one. I saw plenty of cars I *wanted* to buy, but I wasn't *ready* to buy. I wonder if any of the car salespeople ever thought to ask the question, "If you find one you like are you looking to purchase today, next week, next month?" They all were quick to give me their pricing and tell me what a great deal it was, yet none of them asked me what number they'd have to sell it to me for in order for me to buy it that day. Pretty simple question, but when is the last time you had a car guy ask you it? I'm not talking about the cheesy, "What do I need to do to get you in this car today?" question. Just a simple qualification for pricing and what my budget expectations are. Instead I waste their time collecting pricing on the car I want from all different dealers looking for the best deal, and they don't even know it.

The takeaway here is to value your time, it's important. Pricing and solution presentation should be the last step in the process. I always hear the objection of, "They want to know how much it's going to cost them before they will meet with me." If this is the case then throw out ballpark numbers with disclaimers. If I run into one of these pricing hounds I'll throw out that our original analysis could be anywhere between $150,000-$1.2 million depending on the scope of work and deliverables. Put them back in their place by showing them how dumb the question really is. You can't quote a price and expect to win without understanding what their challenge is and the real reason they need the pricing number so quickly. And if you run into this situation I can promise you that you're at the wrong level for decision making.

You should only present the pricing when you are ready to release control of the sales process to your prospect for their internal decision making process. For one of my largest deals I let them know a price range for my services in the beginning of the sales process depending on what the scope of the contract would be. As I walked them down my sales process, if the scope changed I always let them know that the pricing would increase if we added such and such into the scope, or decrease if we took it out. It is important to have your prospect understand your pricing and how it is subject to change based upon the additional work and services you add to it. Remember that your time is valuable and your company resources are just as valuable, so put a monetary number on it. Your prospect does the same for their customers as well.

I leverage my pricing as the last step and to me it's usually the icing on the cake once I've shown them my solution and the services my company offers. Make sure you put the pricing in at the end of your sales process, after you have agreed your solution meets all of their needs. If you have overcome every objection and the prospect has agreed with your solution, then the pricing should be a non-issue, especially if you've given them the proper range in the beginning of the sales process.

A couple of years ago when everyone thought we were going into another great depression and no one was buying, (and by the way this is when I sold the most, remember even in the original Great Depression millions were being sold,) one of my customers called me with the most ridiculous request. They asked us to cut 10% off of our bill, while keeping the same services. They were asking this of all their partners/contractors and vendors across the board. So here's how this really went down. The CEO/CFO looked at the numbers as a whole and noticed in Q3 they were way behind. The quickest way to catch up would be to cut expenditures by 10%; it was a "let's go beat the shit out of our vendors to get a better discount if they still want to do business with us" approach. This is a classic example of what I was talking about earlier; the C-Level says "Make it happen!" (no detail, just cut expenditures by 10%.) When that message gets down to the Director level it's interpreted as "Go beat and threaten our vendors."

In this case every other vendor was signing off on it and taking a hit for their company. My company was going through a tough time so I made a pretty ballsy play which ended up working out well. I met with the VP and Director of the company, they were my day-to-day contacts in this large account when I sold it about three years earlier. I had been trying to branch out and expand outside of our existing services to them for quite some time, but could never get traction or momentum to move forward. I met with them, but instead of folding like every other vendor or partner they had, I stood my ground. I told them that I couldn't save them an additional 10% off the existing services, but I could save them 40% in their AP/AR department and 23% in their Supply Chain management. I had a frank conversation with them and told them that if they really wanted to save money, let's talk. If they were just looking to hit a number from the top then I told them to keep going back to the other vendors. Everyone at my company thought it was a horrible play; I was going to lose the account, on and on and on. About two days later, the VP called and said he wanted me to show them how I could do this with his boss in attendance. You better believe I had some bridge the gap and validation meetings with them.

The moral of the story is that they contacted me wanting me to cut 10% off my existing contract, and 5 months later they had signed an additional $2.5 million a year in revenue with my company. It all boils down to how you are going to position yourself and your pricing. Hopefully this has given you some ideas to apply to your situation, and while I know hope is not a strategy, I wanted to give my insight to the whole pricing debate.

12

Referral Dos & Don'ts

Getting a referral from a customer is the best type of marketing you can do for yourself. When a customer has enough faith in you to divulge another potential prospect to you, only good things can happen. The problem is that most people, especially the 97%, either don't ask for a referral or don't know the right way to do it. Think about all of the customers you have signed up recently or in the past. If you're an old timer, keep thinking, back before cell phones. Now think about how many of those customers actually gave you a viable referral which turned into a lead? Pretty scary, right? You're probably either not doing it at all or you're doing it the wrong way.

One time I did a call with a Jr. Sales rep on an account he had lost in a competitive situation. I made him schedule a Win/Loss call (see Chapter 13) and gave him a list of questions to ask the prospect on why he was unable to secure their business. During the call he asked the prospect for a referral. I was shocked! Here we were asking her why we weren't able to close her and he had the audacity to ask her if she knew anyone else she could recommend who might want to do business with us. It was painful, to say the least. And guess what her response was? I thought this was common sense; if you're going to ask, you certainly don't ask the person who just told you no. But the more I paid attention, the more I noticed that salespeople really don't know how or when to ask for the referral.

Another mistake I see all the time is when salespeople ask for the referral too early in the process. Most salespeople will ask for the referral right after the close of the sale, before they have even proven the worth of the sale and earned the right to ask for the referral. I think we are all guilty of this misstep in our career at one point or another. We are so excited about securing the sale and closing it that we feel the momentum and timing are right to ask if they know of anyone else who could benefit from our services. In the long run, though, this rarely pans out.

Networking groups are another dead-end. How many that you have been involved with have actually produced a sale for you? I remember when I made the mistake of getting into sales management; I know, I was young and dumb and believed the whole corporate ladder thing, but I realized it was babysitting, reporting and making less money, so I quickly got back into sales. I need to be in control of my own destiny. Anyway, back when I was a sales manager one thing I would ask when interviewing was, "What type of organizations do you belong to and how do you network with them?" What I was looking for were people to say they go to Chamber of Commerce meetings. These were the poster children of bad salespeople. It's a breakfast group that meets monthly; talk about a group where there are more realtors there than anyone else! You quickly realize it's full of salespeople who don't want to go out and find business, but would rather pretend that they're at appointments by attending this breakfast.

The same goes for referrals; don't pretend to be asking for something and half ass it. Referrals can be a huge advantage for you in getting into another account. Earlier I gave you a tip about mapping out the Board of Directors in corporate accounts. Can you imagine if you had a board member refer you and push you towards the other members who all sit on the boards of other Fortune 500 companies, or better yet are the CEOs of these other companies? I've had it happen personally, and it is a thing of beauty. If you do your piece of the business correctly and you differentiate yourself from everyone else then you can typically live off of the referrals for new business. When you get your sales funnel up to this level, your sales job turns out to be a cake walk.

As salespeople this is generally what we are looking for: the least amount of work for the most amount of money. It's a common theme. Great salespeople put in a tremendous amount of work, but they work smart and efficiently rather than cold calling forty doors a day. That old school model will phase out over the years, especially with the new security requirements most buildings have now. So if salespeople could work the least amount and make the most money by referrals, why don't they leverage this more often? The answer is that they don't know how to, because no one has ever shown them a good way to ask for a referral or even how to know when the right time is to ask for one.

So when is the right time to ask for a referral? **You want to ask for a referral after you have delivered on what you sold them and the customer is happy with your complete process**. In my line of sales, I typically ask for the referral at our quarterly review meeting *after* implementation and the numbers have all matched up with what I presented during the sales process. If this all adds up and the customer feels the transition was smooth, I will then have a direct conversation with them about referrals.

As you know, asking for referrals can be tough. It is sometimes an awkward question to ask and it requires your customer to do a lot of thinking. **Take the thinking out of it for them**. It's like the difference between asking an essay question or a multiple choice question. If you ask the question, "Do you know anyone else who can use my services?" you are asking for the essay question answer. And what can someone typically do in an essay question better than any other question? Bullshit. You can add all types of fluff to your answer and never really answer the question. Politicians are the best at turning any question they get, even a yes or no question, into an essay response.

So how do you ask for a referral? You have to play into two very strong human attributes. First, people like to be asked questions to which they know the answer. Second, people generally like to be helpful if it doesn't require too much effort on their part and they are convinced you would do a good job representing their sponsorship. People buy from people they like and trust. People refer people they trust. And just like everything I have talked about in this book, the best way to get a referral is to do the proper prep work beforehand. I've done this so well that one of my customers actually turned into what seemed like a rep for me every time he attended a tradeshow, conference, and even chance meetings with people on a plane. Just like the best told jokes, it's all in the delivery and prep work.

By the time you're asking for a referral from your customer you should already have an excellent rapport built with them, so asking should be really easy and I'll show you how to position it so it's not awkward. Just like multiple choice questions, you want to give them names they may know. This requires you to do your research. Find out what groups they belong to, what companies belong to them, what tradeshows/conferences/training seminars they attend, what other companies attend them, what companies they used to work for, etc. Look on social media sites like LinkedIn to see with whom they're connected. Have names of people you are trying to get a meeting with who could be connected to your customer possibly through six degrees of separation (and don't forget to tie them back to Kevin Bacon.) The better the names you give them the more chance you'll have that they know them and then this can also get the wheels turning for them of other names they know.

Remember what you put into it is what you will get out of it. I'm a firm believer that if you have delivered on everything you said you would and the customer is happy, you have earned the right to ask for a referral. In this same context, you also have the duty to your customer to make this process a no-brainer for them and as painless as possible.

I'm always against scripts, but I'll give you a baseline you can use when asking for a referral. As with everything, it all depends on the situation. There is no one magic way to do it, but this gives you an example of what I often say to my customers. I structure my request for referral in a very honest and simple way:

> "Larry, I wanted to ask for your help in coaching me through something, because of the work we have done and the good relationship we have built with you and your company. I have targeted companies in your industry from a prospecting standpoint and I have hit a wall getting in to see some of them that I think you may know. I'd like to run a few names by you and see if you can point me in the right direction or give me guidance with any of them. Is this ok? I know you just got back from the trade show in Vegas, ABC Company was there as well, do you know your counterpart from this company Mike Rogers, or could you give me some direction on him or his company? I know you came over here from XYZ Company, do you know Cindy Miller,

was she in your department when you were there? Any guidance on this one?"

Keep feeding your customer different names. Typically when you feed them names, even if they don't know any of them, (which is very common so don't get discouraged,) they *will* want to tell you about someone they *do* know. This is the helpful human nature thing. I've actually asked one of my customers about three or four names I knew he probably didn't know, and this guy was pretty much a hard ass and a hard guy to deal with. After the fourth name he didn't recognize he said, "Hold on, I don't know any of these people, if you want to talk to someone you should meet Rick at ABC Company, I'm doing lunch with him next week." This is what you are looking for, that one in. I got it even from the hard ass himself, so I know this method works.

Now here is the key on how to end whichever approach you use to ask for referrals, and YOU MUST DO THIS AT THE END EVERY TIME!!! Again, I hate scripts, but this is to demonstrate what you have to ask at the end:

> "This has been very helpful, Larry (even if it hasn't) am I missing any obvious ones in your mind that I could possibly contact?"

HERE'S YOUR TIP OF THE WEEK BONUS, YOU MUST SAY THIS EVERY TIME:

> "Thanks again, Larry. I really appreciate your guidance on these. Do you mind if, in the future, I give you an occasional call like this and run some names by you?"

You have now set it up to pump him for referrals moving forward. You can also use this as a different perspective in trying to penetrate other accounts similar to his. You can gain tremendous insight into his company while he's helping you get into another company. For example, I will call my customer back later after the original meeting and tell him I'm running into a problem getting over a certain title's head or getting to a certain person in another company. Without fail, they always tell me about the internal politics in their own company when they're trying to help me. They'll say things like, "I know here it would have to go to Mark first and then he would push it down, but Steve always sits on the board in finance so you may want to try and get in with Finance." It's a thing of beauty when it works, because you're also getting more information into the internal processes of your existing customer even as he's helping you with a future prospect.

By setting up your customer for the OK to run names by him in the future, you have also set him up to be used as a reference call for your potential prospects. Do you see how I'm three steps ahead of where you thought this was going? Think about it, what happens if you find a name he knows and you start engaging that person as a prospect? During the sales cycle, how much of an advantage would it be for you to say, "Please call Larry over at X Company, he'd love to catch up and tell you about the work we did for him."

Remember to stay professional and structured with this approach. If your customer gives you a name, be courteous and update them on it. The worst thing you can do is not let them know how it panned out. If people give you something, especially help, they want to hear if it helped out or not. It's human nature. Make sure you always let them know where it stands. This can only help you, and it never hurts you. I've gone back to one of my customers before and told them thanks for giving me Cindy's name, I've left her a couple of messages, but haven't received a return call. I've literally had the customer bring me into his office and watch as he typed her an email to give me a call. Like I said, this can only help and shouldn't hurt you.

Don't forget that prep work and knowledge are key in everything; you should be noticing a recurring theme by now. Your referral base will be your top prospect base for new customers; put the time into referrals, you'll work less and make more.

13

I'm Out

I analyze everything so I can learn from my mistakes and get better. This includes analyzing how I did with each deal. If you lose a deal, do you perform a Win/Loss report after every opportunity? It takes discipline to follow through with it, but it can really help you understand from the customer's perspective what worked and what didn't. I've heard some of my best constructive criticism by doing this, and eaten some of the best humble pie you can get for free! It's one of the hardest and most frustrating feelings when you have gone on a long journey with a prospect and for whatever reason they elect not to move forward with your sale. Most of us have been there more often than in the victory circle. The key is to learn from it.

I've found that after spending considerable time with you, the prospect will share information they didn't disclose during the sales process. It would have been nice if they shared earlier, but it never works that way; remember they keep everything close to the chest for you to figure out on your own. Time to make lemons into a high proof blended cocktail of hard lemonade! After I receive the bad news it's always helps to remember that it's actually *their* mistake. I truly believe my solution is the best solution for the customer and if they choose not to select me then they have made a poor decision for their company.

If I lose the sale at a lower level I'll sometimes go up to a higher level on an issue which may have come up, or let them know that their staff needs to view this initiative at the macro level and not just departmentally as they're currently doing. You have to be careful with this approach and word it properly. I sometimes send a thank you letter to the executives for allowing us to participate in the project. I let them know we won't be moving forward due to the team members looking to take a more centralized departmental approach compared to the enterprise solution my company is used to providing (if I'm lucky and we service some of their competitors I'll list them here.) This has worked in getting an additional meeting or a clarification meeting as a follow up, but it has only secured me one additional deal so far. The key is to be careful how you position it, you don't want to piss them off so badly that you can't do business with them in the future. Keep it very factual and to the point, short and sweet. Like I said, this can be a risky approach.

For every account I do a Win/Loss report. This is a phone interview I have with my prospect to help me better position myself and my company for the next opportunity in their particular field of business. Most prospects you have lost will do this, outside of an RFP environment. The key to the Win/Loss call is to ask questions which will help you on future endeavors. Leave your pride at the door and don't be defensive. Ask very conceptual questions about how you got into the account, which approaches they liked, didn't like, etc. Ask about you as a salesperson, and have them rate you compared to other salespeople they use. You've already lost it, so have fun with it now, you have the right to at least laugh about it. I sometimes share with the prospect some crazy assumptions I had about their team members. I'll let them know that to me, Cindy seemed really defensive and I thought she was the saboteur, etc. This is when you can sharpen your sales skills to see how accurate you really were in reading all the people involved.

Before you conduct the Win/Loss call write down the reasons they initially stated as to why you didn't win the sale. They always give the boilerplate response to sales reps, but when you dig deeper you'll find the real reason. Prior to the call, it's important to write down the reason they gave you, but also write down what *you* think the reason is they didn't buy from you.

During the call you should position your questioning in the best, most appropriate way. The purpose of the Win/Loss call is to get them to answer the question "why didn't you choose us?" without having to ask that outright. They feel they've already answered that question with their boilerplate response, so you have to find creative ways to get to the real answer. Here are some examples of how to structure the questions:

- Where do you feel the best "value" of my company was?
- Where was the least?
- What areas did you feel we addressed the strongest?
- What areas did you feel were the weakest in our presentation?
- If you were my coach, what would be the one thing you would tell me to practice on or work on more for future bids?
- What were your internal deciding factors? Please list them in importance.
- What specifically about my sales presentation did you like/dislike?
- If I were going on an interview what would you tell me to highlight from my skill set, and what should I stay away from?

These questions tend to give prospects diarrhea of the mouth; once you ask them the prospects tend to talk and talk. The other component of this is the human factor; people don't generally like to tell others straight to their face what they don't like about them or what they didn't like about their sale. These questions get them out of their comfort zone and so they tend to talk a TON. This is great, though you will have to pick through some of the standard language used and filter the misinformation. You can usually figure out where you went wrong in the sales process by reading between the lines. If you didn't follow every step as a foundation like I have outlined in this book, chances are one of those missteps is a contributing factor.

The goal of the Win/Loss report is for you as a salesperson to realize what your strengths and weaknesses are, and where you could have helped the sales process further towards the close position. I typically take the information I get from the phone call and look for key words or something I may have said which could have altered the prospect's decision process in choosing me. The key is to be honest with yourself and take the constructive criticism to heart. It is amazing how you can think you won or lost a deal based upon your perception and then you find out your prospect selected you for completely different reasons. This is the most valuable information you can obtain from your prospect.

Find out the real reason they selected you or the real reason they elected not to move forward with your solution.

It is important for you to constantly learn and grow as a salesperson. The markets and companies are changing just quickly, and decision making criteria is constantly evolving. You need to make sure you are at the front of each and every curve rather than playing catch up. These calls can help you change the way you are perceived in the marketplace. Use this exercise to make it more formal for the prospect so they have to put some thought into answering your questions. It's a great self-training method that can be used to help even the most experienced sales professional.

14

WATCH YOUR BACK

Now that we've taken a look at all the steps in the sales process, let's talk about some of the obstacles you will encounter as you get your real sales on. When you're king of the mountain everyone is going to try and knock you down, it's human nature. It's why our society hates the super-rich, and why we think they should be taxed more because they make more. This is the "I don't have, so you shouldn't either" mentality. When you get to be the top salesperson you'll find you have to battle many political forces which you may or may not see trying to topple you.

INTERNAL POLITICS

A majority of the problems come from other salespeople within your own organization. These are the player-haters. They're not number one, and they think you have it easy (right or wrong, shouldn't matter.)

When I became the top producer in my company with my first sales job, I started doing what most top producers do, carrying the big stick and seeing what I could get away with. We had morning sales meetings every Monday at 7:00AM. I'm a huge NFL football nut, so back in my younger days right out of college it was very common to catch me doing an all-day drinking binge on Sundays, and watching every game at the bar with ten to fifteen of my closest friends. Monday morning 7:00AM would always come way too early for me, and definitely too early to be effective in any way. Once I became number one in the company for billed sales revenue, I started to elect not to attend the mandatory Monday morning sales meetings (you have to love the balls of salespeople.)

My boss at the time was Mr. D, and he was okay with this. He got word from Human Resources that other salespeople were complaining that it was unfair they had to be at the meetings when I didn't. Mr. D was always the type of guy who looked out for his top producers, and let's face it, I was the one paying his mortgage with my sales. He called a mandatory sales meeting and let everyone know about the complaints placed to Human Resources about my absences from the Monday morning sales meetings. I thought for sure my days of missing Monday meetings were over, but he did the most incredible thing I still remember to this day. Mr. D let everyone know, "When you're at your number, I'm Stevie Wonder." He was saying that if you met your sales number you could get away with stuff the other salespeople couldn't. In one sentence he made the player-haters feel as they should, weak, and his top producer feel even more confident that his boss would go to bat for him under any circumstance. Amazing!

One of the other sales reps challenged him, and this was someone who is probably now in marketing telling other salespeople he used to be in sales. Mr. D quickly squashed him with, "Oh, you think it's unfair, then let's go to the videotape, the numbers don't lie." I knew that "going to the videotape" meant pulling up the month's billed revenue per sales rep, a category I was dominating in throughout the company nationwide. Mr. D began to shred the guy's numbers and let him know he should be more concerned about *his* numbers and sales rather than *my* attendance record. Mr. D totaled his nine months of billed revenue and put it against my fifteen-day running billed average; I toasted him by over 421%. It was at this moment I realized when everyone is nice to your face or says congrats to you, some are behind the scenes player-hating; if they can't be successful then you shouldn't either.

You may also see this when you close one of the biggest sales in company history; this is when they really come out of the woodwork. This will be when people try to take credit for selling your deal. All of a sudden every name wants to be attached to your deal. I'm a big proponent of giving credit where credit is due, but you have to watch out for the leeches.

I worked for a global Japanese company and the American division was king of this model. We'd have a WebEx or conference call with a large client and all of a sudden we outnumbered the customer on the conference call five to one. You need to challenge this as much as possible. I've had very hard conversations with people who feel that since they were part of a meeting or attended a call they should be associated with the selling of the deal. They were there but made no contribution whatsoever. Think about how many times your sales manager or VP is on a call and knows nothing about the client, strategy, purpose of the call, etc. These are the people that instantly cause you credibility issues as the industry expert in your sales process.

When everyone and their brother wants to be on one of your calls, here are some quick questions you can ask them which will generally put them in their place in a nice, politically correct way:

- What do you think the purpose of the call should be?
- What role will you take during the call to leverage the overall strategy?
- What is the value of you being on the call?
- What objections do you think they will have with our proposal?
- What questions will be directed towards you, in particular?
- What do you know about the opportunity?
- What do you think we are selling them?

These are simple basic questions you will know the answers to, if you're a real salesperson. You'll be amazed at how these basic questions will allow other people trying to get on the call or into the meeting realize that they have no business being there. As I've mentioned before, you should always have a relevant reason to contact your prospect or customer. Having multiple people on a call just to have them on a call will hurt the overall impression you give to the customer. Remember, one person's perception is another's reality. You will have to educate your coworkers on what their particular role is on any sales call. You are the expert and the salesperson who dictates the overall strategy of the call and the account.

Executive Politics

When selling corporate accounts you will always and in every aspect run into politics. It's the name of the game in some accounts with internal battling, strong-arming, and negotiations; you name it and these accounts have it. It is important to understand what these factors are in order to achieve or move your prospect towards the close column. Let's be honest, the reason there are so many politics is that most people are looking to get ahead or move up the corporate ladder and others are protecting what they view as theirs. I see this all the time; corporations are like dysfunctional families, and it's a wonder they are in business considering how the lower or middle management and departmental levels are run.

It's always funny to hear a C-Level executive talk about one of their initiatives on the phone to shareholders. They make the project or vision seem so advanced and give the impression it's working seamlessly. But when you come on site and do an analysis of the day-to-day operations, this couldn't be further from the truth. So why is this? It's due to executive politics and to most of the players not wanting to bring attention to the fact that their department or division is not running well. Real leaders will step up and say, "This is not working right, our process is wrong." Unfortunately there are not many true leaders out there in the business world. In corporations, the bigger the organization the bigger this challenge is. As a salesperson you must be aware of this.

I've seen people come in recommending huge software systems to rival Oracle, PeopleSoft, SAP, etc. They present their solution as a replacement to these large multi-million dollar investments to the same people who chose them in the first place. How far do you think their sale will go when all they do each time they present is give their prospect a black eye? Not far at all.

On the flip side, you have the business owner of this problem trying to hide the fact that they are having challenges by hiring or buying something from you that will compliment or strengthen this weakness. In the software world this is where middleware comes in. While you may get a sale out of this, you must weigh all the pros and cons of each opportunity. As mentioned before, no two sales are alike, every opportunity is different and every circumstance is different.

Humans are protective creatures by nature, so are SVP's, VP's, Directors, Managers, etc. The lower down the food chain you go in a corporate environment, the more protective they are. Think of it as a formal dinner party. A large dinner table is set and everyone has a plate of food in front of them. At the head of the table you have the C-level executive (CEO/CFO/CIO/COO/etc.) They are sitting back in their chair away from the plate of food schmoozing and boozing, laughing and having a good time. Next to them you have the EVP or SVP sitting more formally in their chair, but engaged in the conversation with napkin on their lap. Next to them you have the VP level, sitting upright in their chair, hands folded nicely on the table, observing what the big boys are doing and trying to listen in on the conversation. Next to them you have the Director level, they've already started to reach for the bread and eat their food, looking up occasionally to make sure the conversation is not about them. Next to them you have the Manager level, they're already eating, with their hands around the plate protecting it. They're also ordering the most expensive liquor from the bar, not because they like it, but because it's free and they want expensive. They are not engaged with anyone but themselves, the "I'm going to get mine while the getting is good" mentality. Off in the corner away from the table is some procurement guy, awkward and not involved in any sense, but he has to be there because it's company policy. And the sales guys? They are, I'm sure, at the bar breaking about a hundred different HR rules and completely oblivious to what time dinner started. Typical, right?

This may seem like a crazy analogy, but think about your prospects and the people with titles you deal with in your accounts, I'm not that far off base, am I? The higher up the food chain you go the easier it is to have a conceptual conversation. The lower down the food chain is where you will run into departmental, defensive posturing and the lack of ability to see the big picture. This is why I always try to stay high and will walk away from opportunities that deal with the lower titles. Remember details are done at the lower section of the hierarchy of a corporate organization. Corporate politics is something you will have to learn in your company and in your prospects. The key is to sit as close to the head of the table to eat and get involved in the conversation by doing your research and understanding the audience in attendance

Because politics plays such a key role in the larger deals, it's something you can't avoid. Make sure if you're picking sides, you pick the one that's going to win. I learned this the hard way and picked someone one time who originally signed a contract with me, then they had an internal power struggle. I chose my side being loyal to the person who originally signed with me, but in the end he lost that power struggle and I was out of the contract two months later. After this I vowed never to choose sides again. Now I'm Switzerland in terms of the internal battle, or I'll give the perception I am and help the one to whom I'm loyal on the side.

Web Presence

You should also be careful about the personal information you send out into cyberspace. You won't find a lot of information out there about executives in the Fortune 500 space, and you should be the same way. Check those Facebook and LinkedIn pages. If you are presenting yourself as a professional who is the best in your industry, then that needs to show up in your web presence as well. If you have a webpage or personal profile with pictures of you partying and hanging out or complaining about your company, people will find it easily via a search engine. Do you want that to be your prospect? I had a customer one time tell me they looked up their other sales rep on Facebook, only to find that he was complaining about his company's implementation and how they hadn't been paid proper commissions on their last deal. Can you imagine that? Needless to say the rep did not secure their business and probably has no idea why. Keep the search fields on yourself as professional as possible.

Also consider the email you're writing before you click "send." I was once told to never write an email I wouldn't want shown as a top news story on every channel. This may make you want to recall a ton of emails, but it is good advice. Just imagine that everything you send into cyberspace is something that could be seen by your prospect.

There are politics in every company, make sure you are aware of the forces both outside of your control and the ones you can control. "You're only as good as your last deal" is a great methodology to follow. Don't be the old-timer in your company who sold one big deal in his life and that's all they can talk about; the one hit wonder syndrome. Leverage your skill set to separate yourself from your internal competition and colleagues. When you're doing well remember that not everyone would like you to continue to succeed. This is especially true when you start with a new organization. Keep your nose clean and your head down and concentrate on what you can do for your customers. Remember, it's always your customer first, company second. If you have major internal politics within your own company then focus more on your customers and prospects and let the other stuff fall to the wayside

15

Value Your Time

I've talked throughout the book about how important it is to value your time. Knowing how you spend your time and the right way to spend your time can make all the difference in the world on how successful you will be in sales. In sales there are several ways you can ensure your time is used wisely and efficiently. As I mentioned earlier, one of the biggest ways is to know when to walk away from an opportunity. Don't waste your time on unclosable opportunities. This is the biggest challenge salespeople face, moving on or putting a prospect out to pasture. The bigger the account, the harder it is for salespeople to do this. As the salesperson, you need to figure out when it's worth your time to pursue a prospect and when it's best to walk away.

You also need to understand what other sales tasks within your own company are worth your time. The bigger the company you work for the more bullshit you'll have to do in day-to-day operations for sales. This is just how it is. The company you sell for might be so big that the left doesn't talk to the right, and the salespeople have to put up with way too many administrative tasks. If you work at a large company think about how many reports, logs, updates to funnels, one-on-ones, weekly conference calls, etc., you have to do. This can be a full time job in and of itself. At what point do you decide you're wasting your time completing all of these reports and weekly updates? At what point do you realize how much time, energy, resources, and value this wastes on your end? There is no one answer for this, all I can recommend is that you take the time to understand where your top priorities are and how you can obtain your goals.

As a sales rep one of your biggest challenges can be your own company wasting the most amount of your time. You have to be extremely cautious of this model and falling into it. Doing weekly sales calls with your team, where you just go over what you did for the week, does this really help? The answer is no, this is probably the biggest waste of time, yet every company has these weekly sales calls to go over what each sales person did for the week. What companies fail to realize is that they are now taking seven to eight revenue-generating positions and having them be stagnant, listening to updates their sales manager needs in order to update the higher levels of the food chain. This model baffles me every time.

Sales is an individual sport, much like high school wrestling. Sure, you hope your high school wins, but when it comes down to it, it's just you out on the mat wrestling another person, very individual. Much like sales, you get paid on what you sell and you have an individual quota. You do not get bonuses if the entire sales team overachieves. So why would you care what the other salespeople have done for the week? I understand if the spirit of the calls is to share information and have it be a collaborative meeting, however 99.9% of the time this is not the case. Typically the person running the call starts it off with, "Who wants to go first?" You then have to stay on the line while they go down the seven or eight other people in order to get to your week, which you've probably already logged or reported it in some other manner. But you still have to go through all this, every week.

This to me is a great example of how to not use your time, value it more. I've had conversations with my VP's on these calls, telling them I can send them what they need or they can call me individually to get the information. This cuts down my calls from one to two hours to fifteen or twenty minutes. It's a huge time saver and puts me back in the field quicker. I'm all about being a team player, so if they structured the call around strategy in penetrating accounts, best practices, etc. I'm all for it. But the truth is those calls are hard to come by when you get into the day-to-day or week-to-week operations of a sales company.

When you make a stand against your company in relation to the usage of your time, the immediate push back will be great. They may even use the team player line on you. One time I worked for a company and they wanted me to take time out of my day to help show the other salespeople what I've been doing to be so much more successful than everyone else. I refused unless they paid me more (my time is valuable, I know it down to the hourly rate, do you?) My VP, the same who would fire you the minute you weren't at your quarterly number said to me, "There's no 'I' in team, Bryan. Be a team player and help the other guys get to your level." Most people would have done it, but that's the beauty about being the rock star in sales, you get away with murder. My response…"No, and just so you know, there's two 'I's in commission." Know when to say, "Enough of the madness and let me sell."

Putting value on your time means understanding exactly what your time is worth. As a salesperson you should be able to calculate your close ratio. How many calls or contacts do you have to make prior to getting an appointment? How many appointments do you have to go on before getting a sale? Once you know your close ratio you can better understand how much time you have to put in for each sale. Most salespeople don't even know this simple number. You should be able to rattle it off to someone. Go by your last year's numbers, it's a great way to shut people down when you say, "I have a 67% close ratio, what's yours?" They won't know it, so you have to.

Once you have your close ratio number, you can then also figure out how much you are worth an hour. You have to understand this number so you can know when to walk away from a prospect and quantify it better. Take what you made last year, I take this annual amount and then divide it by twelve. Once I have this monthly number I will divide this number by 173.33 (hours in a month). I now have my hourly rate and worth. It's not an exact science, but it will give you a good idea of what you would get paid if it were hourly. Now that I know this I can figure out if taking time out of my day to respond to an RFI is worth my time (Nope.) If it would take me two hours to complete an RFI response, and let's say I'm worth $834/hour, is it worth $1600 to respond to an RFI? Would I pay $1600 out of my pocket to respond to an RFI?? These are great questions to ask yourself.

What happens is you start to realize opportunities or things your company wanted you to do, you wouldn't if you had to cut a check out of your hourly rate to do them. This is the essence of valuing your time and knowing when doing something is not worth the effort or your money. This is vital for success in sales.

16

Final Thoughts

I wrote this book because I was tired of all the fluff sales books out there. This book is not intended for the rookie sales rep, or the bad sales rep. It was written for the other outstanding salespeople out there who work hard every day to provide an exceptional experience for their customers. The best salespeople always have and always will put their customer above everything else and will do so with the highest integrity and morals. I was just so sick of sales books being written by people who aren't even in sales anymore, they're just marketing themselves personally and their books. I view them as old washed up guys who probably did well back in the day, but times have changed, companies have changed, and the way you sell has changed. Welcome to the 21st Century of sales.

I was tired of no one properly explaining what to do to get into, work, and close big accounts. Everyone just talks about conceptual fluff and common sense. Give me a list of Fortune 20 accounts where I have no established relationships within the account and I would go up against any salesperson out there peddling their books, seminars, training or whatever, and show you who is in "real sales." Why? **Because I'm still selling**. I'm calling on accounts every day just like you. When you're done reading this book, I'm still making calls because I'm a real sales guy, just like you. I have great sales stories to share from last week, not 1982. That's the big difference here.

As I've mentioned before, there is no one way to sell, no magic paint brush which will work for every deal, every industry and every sale. It just doesn't happen this way. As a salesperson you must constantly strive to learn more and be better. Remember, you want to be the best not only in your company, but in your industry as a whole. Sales is the hardest job out there and has the least amount of job security, you're only as good as your last deal. I want you to take bits and pieces of what's in this book and use whatever you think can help you in moving the sale you're working towards the close. It's up to you to decide what is relevant and will or will not work in your particular sale; you are the salesperson who drives the strategy and knows what's best for your customer.

We salespeople are always closest to the deal. While your CEO's/VP's and managers may have good insight and recommendations on how to handle the sale, keep them as just that: recommendations. It is good to have another person look at your opportunity because they aren't as close to it and can give you a different perspective, but don't let them tell you how it should be sold if they have never met the customer. Take pride in the fact that you are a sales professional. Try to get to the 3% of all salespeople, then earn it and stay there. And if after reading this book you still didn't grasp anything, well, there's always marketing.

PRAISE FOR THE AUTHOR

For those of you who wrote these kind words about me and didn't even know I was writing a book, here's my shout out back to ya:

"Bryan Seck doesn't sell anything... he paints a picture about what the solution can be, how it can be implemented and lets the client beg him to provide it! Bryan has an aptitude to gain the confidence of C-Level leadership and understand their business needs while crafting a solution to ensure their and his success. He is able to guide project teams, direct technical staff and bring together a cohesive end product. Bryan encapsulates the best in "solutions selling." - **Pat Mustico, Vice President, Sales**

"I had the privilege to work with Bryan over the past years in the capacity as manager and colleague. Bryan is hands down the best sales person I have worked with during my 25 years career with Ricoh. He is intelligent, trustworthy, has high energy, and a burning desire to be the best. His understanding of the C – Level enables him to sell the dream or vision of what he is offering to his customer. He is a proven leader who owns the sales process and guides the customer down the path to a great sale and partnership for life." - **Bill Brady, Regional Sales Director**

"Bryan is an outstanding employee and person. He was a top producer on my team and at our global organization. As the VP of Sales I was able to observe Bryan on a daily and weekly basis. Bryan is a self-starter who is willing to take the lead on any project put before him each & every time and delivered with outstanding results. Bryan understood how to get into C-Level in Fortune 500 accounts and bring them to our largest closed sales in company history. He is an asset to any organization. Whatever he's doing, learn from it and use it!" - **Jack Hawkins, Senior Vice President of Sales**

"I have worked with Bryan on several large projects over the years and Bryan's expertise and professionalism have contributed greatly to the success of the projects. Bryan has a sharp eye for the details of uncovering a client's needs and has a great ability to develop the trust relationship needed to move projects forward with C- level executives." - **Martin Gundel, Enterprise Solutions Consultant**

"I have been very fortunate to work with Bryan throughout the life of many sales cycles. His desire to win is only exceeded by his ability to understand the customer's need and craft the appropriate solution to their problems. He is tenacious in gaining appointments with the appropriate C-Level to articulate the value proposition and develop relationships. His desire to understand the prospect's issues has driven him to become a subject matter expert in process automation and he often becomes their trusted advisor in cost reduction and process improvement. Bryan would be a great addition to any team. Plain and simple, he is a winner, a leader and a team player. He is creative and a life-long learner. I'd be proud to be on any team that he is a part." - **Adam LaFayette, Senior Executive Business Development**

"Bryan is an amazing salesperson who is detail oriented and solutions driven. Bryan brings a vision of a better future-state to the table and also has the commitment to ensure the recommended solution transitions to a working operational solution. He is always thinking outside the box and bringing creative solutions to very complex problems. "We can't do that" is not a part of his vocabulary as he always figures out a way to meet and exceed customer expectations. In addition, he is an outstanding communicator and works well with all levels of our organization. It has truly been a privilege to have Bryan Seck handling our work." - **Joe Hashemi, Vice President, Corporate Services**

"Bryan Seck is a rare sales professional--he is pensive, an excellent listener, and detail oriented. Bryan's success is built on multiple long-term relationships with clients who trust his judgment and respect his values. Bryan takes a long-term approach to account management, inspiring confidence with clients and peers alike. When Bryan undertakes a project, he already has the end and outcome in mind. He will not stop until the goal is reached and everyone is satisfied. Bryan's assets are his diligence, integrity and perseverance, qualities admired by clients and employers equally. I would hire Bryan to work in any company in any capacity. His superior intelligence enables him to adapt quickly, and is also the source of his quick and sometimes mischievous wit." - **Becky Guillory, Global Sales Trainer**

"Bryan has what I would deem the complete 'package' in a sales professional: high-energy, intelligent, gets up to speed incredibly fast, and the absolute desire to achieve. He learned more about this industry (professional services) in the first three months than most learn in 3 years. Some of his best traits are: thinking intelligently on his feet in front of customers, creating successful sales strategies that significantly improve our customer's odds of closing the deal, a great personality and truly caring about the service his customers are receiving. Not to offer up a cliché, but Bryan is the epitome of a team player, and will work as many hours as it takes to close a deal. It is a real pleasure working with a true professional such as Bryan." - **John Flikeid, Strategic Planner**

"Bryan Seck is the rare combination of heart, talent, and intelligence mixed with absolute desire to succeed. In my first sales position, I had the fortunate experience of reporting directly to Bryan at ATX Communications. Bryan took the time to develop me into a top producer, teaching me how to listen, understand and solve issues. Without Bryan's guidance my sales career would have likely ended early and I would be doing something else today. As it has played out, I now own and operate a nationwide, 70 seat sales organization…based in large part from what I learned early on by my direct reports and daily interactions with Bryan Seck. He is a builder of business and relationships. One of the best, you need to know Bryan Seck!"
- **Gordon Newton, President, The Newton Group**

"I reported directly to Bryan at ATX. He is a great person and employee. He was a top producer in direct sales and sales management at ATX. As a top leader, Bryan taught me many of his polished sales skills. He is always enthusiastic and passionate throughout the sales process. Bryan always execeeded expectations and is an asset to any organization." - **William Deaton, Account Executive**

"Bryan is one of the most complete sales people I have ever worked with. He is innovative in the way he conducts his business and provides solutions to his customers and constantly seeking to create a better solution. Bryan has consistently achieved the highest results in his position." – **David Faries, Global Account Manager**

"Bryan's intensity and attention to detail set him apart from his peers. He faces challenges head on and turns them into victories. I have had the pleasure of working with him on some high profile engagements and he is the consummate professional. I would recommend Bryan's work without hesitation." - **Frank Elchert, MS, PMP, SSGB**

"Bryan is a dynamic and skilled sales professional who cares about helping his customers achieve their financial bottom line result. I had the honor of working with him during my early years at a large global company. He's a creative thinker with a sharp sense of business drive to get the job done right. He is also a very friendly and supportive colleague which you can count on to get help when you need it. His dynamic and good sense of humor contributed quite a lot to corporate activities and achieving his personal and customer's goals." - **Cuong Dao, Global Executive Vice President**

"I met Bryan in 2008 through a Senior Executive who oversees shared services for a managed health care company. I was told that because of Bryan's unique problem solving skills, he helped the company deliver over $18MM in savings over 3 years and improved relations with their customers. In a very short period of time, he has grasped the key business issues of our field and is uncovering new ways to help our clients and prospects. I have no doubt that Bryan will continue his professional track record of being a superstar performer." – **Richard Hopen, SVP Strategy**

"Over the past 25 years I have had the opportunity to work with a lot of great sales executives and Bryan is definitely at the top of that list. Not only does Bryan have a tremendous work ethic, but he also has the natural ability to build a trusting relationship with his clients. I can say with a lot of confidence that Bryan will be very successful in any Sales Executive position." – **Mark Miller, SVP, Deputy General Manager**

"I hired Bryan and gave him his first job out of college. The first hint that he would be special is that he pursued me with the aggression and professionalism rarely seen by seasoned sales professionals. I actually turned him down 4 times and he kept coming back. I am so happy that he did because this actually became the smartest decision I have ever made in my professional career. Within a relatively short period of time Bryan became a top producing representative who consistently over achieved. In addition he acquired some of the larger opportunities in the company. If I were to start a sales organization Bryan would be at the top of my list." - **Stephen "Mr. D" Dyer, Regional Sales Director**